510 Creative Writing Prompts:
For Aspiring and Experienced Writers

By Jonathan Wright

First Printing.

ISBN-10: 1530099757
ISBN-13: 978-1530099757

Attribution:
Cover Image by James from *GoOnWrite.com*.

Thank you for the support.

Table of Contents

Introduction

The purpose of this book is to inspire and motivate. I want to nudge you towards writing your first story. If you're already an experienced writer, I'd like to help you develop ideas. For aspiring and experienced writers, I hope this book helps you defeat writer's block. The writing prompts will be thorough and creative – more than simple quotes or definitions. Real writing prompts for real writers.

This book is a collection of 510 creative writing prompts. The prompts will range from every genre imaginable – horror, thriller, science-fiction, fantasy, comedy, action and everything in-between. You'll find prompts about time travel, dystopian and post-apocalyptic worlds, espionage, classical horror creatures, aliens, possession, serial killers, embarrassing situations and much more. The purpose is to inspire creativity. Creativity, of course, is key to successful creative writing. (As well as your writing ability, but I digress.)

A single writing prompt may allow you to delve into a great story. Using these prompts, you can create countless scenarios. You can create lively characters and refreshing worlds. Start writing your short story, novelette, novella, novel, blog series, or even a screenplay. Take a prompt and create your story without compromise.

With that said, let's jump into these writing prompts.

102 Creative Writing Prompts

For Aspiring and Experienced Writers

By Jonathan Wright

The Prompts

1. You suspect your nation's leader has been abducted by aliens. You believe he's been body snatched – an alien is now your nation's leader. You present your discovery to nothing but laughter and ridicule. As an important speech approaches, you set out to prove your theory...

2. You are given a special notebook. By drawing in this notebook, you can teleport yourself to any desired location. But, your drawing must be as accurate as possible. What if you're a horrible artist? What misadventures can you explore?

3. You love strategy video games, especially real-time strategy games. In fact, through endless gaming, you've become the top player in the world. When a new world war breaks outs, you are hired as a strategist to beat the enemy...

4. You arrive home to your apartment complex. You're tired from a long day, you just want to relax. After entering the elevator, you find there's a new button marked 0 on the panel. Curious, you click on the elevator and find yourself heading down for hours...

5. You are a slacker. You wake up at noon and grab a bowl of cereal. As you eat, you flip through the channels on your television. Not before long, you find yourself watching the local news. The FBI and

police are surrounding a home. It looks like your house... What have you done? Can you escape?

6. You are a single parent to a 6-year-old daughter. One day, your child unexpectedly passes after a car accident. Every day since her death, your daughter's best friend has come to your house and asks to play with your daughter – even after you've explained life and death to her. The child tells you, "She's not dead, I can still see her..." What do you do?

7. As the human race, we finally create a manageable, human-level artificial intelligence. We place this humanly program in a humanoid robot and allow it to roam free. To our utter surprise, the robot vanishes. Years later, the robot reemerges with an army of androids...

8. Change an urban legend. Dialing 666 will connect you to a special hotline. This hotline allows you to receive tips for your malicious actions; they'll even help you plan your next crime. Need help hiding a body? You've called the right place.

9. Selling your soul to the Devil becomes mainstream. In order to achieve instant-gratification and treasures beyond their wildest beliefs, people sell their souls to Earth-wandering demons. In order to compete, angels are sent to Earth to barter...

10. Write during the wild west. You are a cowboy having a drink with your pals. A hysterical woman

rushes into the bar and says, "They're coming!" You look out the window and see zombie outlaws surrounding the bar. Fortunately for you and your pals, there's a full moon and you have the ability to transform...

11. At 21-years-old, you realize you are immortal. You stop aging and nothing can harm you – nothing can penetrate your skin, not a knife or bullet. Initially, you welcome your newfound immortality. However, after witnessing life-and-death for centuries, you decide you have had enough – you will kill yourself, but how?

12. You aren't the brightest criminal, but you've had some success. In fact, you've robbed the same bank every weekend for the past three months and you've made off with plenty of riches. You realize it's been easy, you don't like that. You begin to believe they're allowing it on purpose... (Perhaps you died during a robbery and you're cursed to rob the same bank.)

13. The human race is facing extinction as the food supply rapidly dwindles and the economy crashes due to overpopulation and rampant crime. One corporation comes up with a bright idea: Criminals won't burden the taxpayer any longer, they'll be used as food...

14. You are an anxious and timid serial killer. You plaster your shy and "innocent" persona on your online dating profile, and the girls fall for it. Really,

you're using the only dating services to stalk and lure young women/men. What happens if you truly fall in love?

15. You are an obnoxious, misbehaving high school student. One day, you are called into the principal's office, but you're certain you didn't do anything wrong. The principal has a secret request: Please "handle" the bully that has been bothering him...

16. You are a detective. You and your partner are set to interrogate a serial killer claiming to be psychic and psycho. You don't believe him. However, when he starts spouting facts about your life and thoughts, you realize you are going up against something unnatural. How can you find the truth?

17. You and a group of friends decide to test an urban legend. You visit an old roadside phone booth and you're dared to dial the number scraped onto the phone. It's said, if you dial this number, you'll be allowed to talk to the dead...

18. You and your distraught lover are lost in the woods. You were searching for a concert location, but you found yourself in a loop of endless roads. You pick-up a hitchhiker claiming to know the woods like the back of her hand. Not before long, you suspect she's leading you to Hell...

19. After a long struggle with writer's block, you rent a lakeside home and plan to relax. You go for a

swim in the sparkling lake – you swim deep down, jokingly hoping to find treasure. When you emerge, you find you have traveled through time.

20. Write from the perspective of a timid elder. While gardening, you find a peculiar insect on one of your flowers. You can't seem to identify it, though, it's like nothing you've ever seen. Every time you visit your garden, the insect grows larger and more menacing... What is it? (Create a vivid description for the insect. This can go anywhere, so feel free to experiment.)

21. A crafty and entrepreneurial drug dealer conjures a new drug. This psychedelic drug allows you to experience Heaven or Hell. The experience is completely dependent on your personality – particularly, your deeds. What type of experience do you have?

22. Despite claiming otherwise, you are arrested for public intoxication. You're tossed into the back of a patrol car by an irritable police office. Considering the officer's annoyed attitude, you begin to believe the cop is a fraud and you've been kidnapped.

23. One day, you find you have superpowers. You have super strength and agility. You can leap over walls and hold your breath for hours. Your skin is impenetrable, even by bullets. You plan on saving your city from the rampant crime. But, the citizens think you're ugly. They think you're so ugly, they

exile you from the city.

24. In an attempt to make the United States the smartest country on the planet, the government revamps the education system. From now on, if you earn any grade below a B, you'll be forced to drop out of school and work in the mines...

25. You feel the blazing sun on your face. You can hear kids running and bickering around you. You hear the seagulls soaring through the sky. You open your eyes and find yourself at the beach. You don't remember the events prior. You try to move, but you find your body has been buried and only your head is protruding from the sand. Even worse, a child with a conniving smile is sitting across from you...

26. Flip a cliché. Write from the perspective of a professional assassin. You cannot stop killing, you have a lust for blood. Instead of personally wanting to quit, like many cliché hitman stories, your frightened employers beg you to quit.

27. You finally work up the courage to ride a terrifying roller coaster. To your utter disappointment, the roller coaster stops at a loop. After several hours of waiting, your stomach grumbles and you can feel the pee slipping... You can't hold it any longer! (Practice your comedy writing.)

28. You are a student. While traveling abroad, you

are murdered. You wake up in your old home. An incorporeal force tells you: "You will wander the Earth until your remains are found and formally buried." In order to find your body, you'll have to find the killer. Who do you enlist to help you? Where do you start your investigation?

29. Professional online gamers are now considered top-tier athletes. They're beloved by the people and they get paid in the millions. Aspiring to be like them, you join a gaming boot camp. What is your experience?

30. You wake up one morning and feel a tremble – you shrug it off as a small earthquake. You proceed with your day and take your dog for a walk at the park. While walking through the park, a strangely dressed man sitting at a park bench catches your eye. As you approach, you notice he's reading a newspaper from the 1970s...

31. While traveling through South Korea, you commit a crime – you were drunk and you murdered someone. Fearing the consequences, you cross the border and enter North Korea. After traveling for miles, you are utterly shocked – you find a futuristic city filled with towering skyscrapers, floating cars, and happy people.

32. Amidst international tension, the enemy of your country has developed and launched a diabolical weapon. The weapon kills, then reanimates its

victims as flesh-eating zombies. The enemy has effectively used your population as a weapon...

33. In the near future, space travel becomes mainstream. In fact, humans and aliens have started colonizing planets. You are a regular Earth pirate, but business is stalling. You decide to become a space pirate – the very first space pirate. What are some of the obstacles you face? What is your first objective? How does it go?

34. You have lived a normal life for 25 years. There were some trials and tribulations, but everything has been fine. One day, you wake up and find you've actually been in a coma for 25 years. That entire life you thought you had was all a dream...

35. An alien race has finally found our planet. They are not malicious, though, they are actually excited to make contact – they dearly respect the human race and our laws. These aliens, however, land in North Korea. Unfortunately, these aliens believe the isolated country's leader is a God among men...

36. You wake up and hear: "Honey, breakfast is ready!" You shamble out of bed and follow the sweet aroma of pungent coffee, tender eggs, and crisp bacon. You enter the kitchen and take a bite of the crispy bacon and a sip of your coffee. Then, the thought hits you – you're not married, you live alone...

37. While traveling abroad, you are attacked by a large beast – your forearms and legs have been chomped. You believe you've been attacked by a werewolf. You're anxious to find the powers you'll receive. To your utter disappointment, you wake up with the limbs of a dog and the torso/head of a human...

38. In the future, fighting sports have evolved to the next level. Contestants fight to the death. If both contestants survive all of the rounds, they are both killed. In dire need of money, you are entering your first fight... Are you prepared?

39. Tired of being lonely, you are purposely bitten by a vampire and given eternal life. You can't wait to be popular and finally find love. Unfortunately, people don't seem to care about your vampire attributes. Despite the popularity of vampires, you are so ugly, people aren't seduced or frightened by you... And you've got an eternity of this...

40. Drugs have been banned throughout the world – a law that is brutishly enforced. No one dares to break the law, not even the cartels. Without their drugs, people find a new form of escapism. People become addicted to sleep.

41. China begins creating large, man-made islands by the dozens as unsinkable naval bases. To fool the international community, they force thousands of civilians to inhabit the makeshift islands. To China's

utter surprise, the people declare themselves independent and deem their country "New China." You are their leader...

42. While waiting at a bus stop, a nervous man claiming to be from the future approaches you and says: "Listen to me, your actions today will cause the apocalypse, don't..." Before he can finish, he's ran over by the bus and killed. How do you proceed with your day?

43. A recluse has shielded himself from the world since the 90s. Since then, he's been playing a popular but outdated life simulating game. When the game and his old computer stop working in 2015, he's forced outside for the first time. Can he use what he learned in the video game to interact with people? Or will it be gibberish?

44. You lead a fairly normal life. One day, you step outside and find everyone weeping uncontrollably. Everyone is hysterically crying. Everyone, except for... you. What has happened? Why aren't you crying?

45. Create a dystopian world exactly one week from your current date. Society is crashing and the human population is rapidly dwindling. An inexplicable disease has killed off most of the population. This fatal disease kills people if they fall asleep. How long can you stay awake in the lawless land?

46. Due to the dangerous waste dumped into the water, the entire ocean becomes hazardous. You and a buddy don't believe the warning. You convince your friend to jump in, you'll follow. Initially, everything was normal. As your friend emerged, his skin began to melt...

47. Write from the perspective of a very angry person. You're so angry, you plan on killing your boss. However, every time you get close, your boss slips through your grasps and you incidentally kill someone else. Not before long, police believe you're a serial killer, despite your intentions. Can you kill your boss before you get caught? Can you stop accidentally killing people? (A horror-comedy prompt.)

48. Thanks to new technologies, a time-traveling company emerges and offers people the ability to travel 3 days into the future for 24 hours – for a steep price. You try out the technology to your utter dismay. While traversing the future, you find you have been murdered. Before your timer runs out, you must solve your murder to avoid it when you return.

49. Although you don't understand the lyrics, you love listening to foreign pop. Your love is so deep, you decide to learn the language. When you learn the language, you find the lyrics aren't what you expected...

50. You fall in love with an older woman you met online. You are from different countries, eras and cultures, but your connection is incredibly strong – you break through barriers of language and your love shines. One day, she abruptly stops contacting you. After months of loneliness, you set out to visit your love in her country to find...

51. How do they fit so many people into those tiny clown cars? Well, it turns out these special cars actually open to a different dimension. A colorful realm populated by clowns. You decide to enter this world.

52. While speaking to a friend, you become angry. You think: This guy's annoying, why won't he leave? Your friend responds, "Because you invited... Oops." You discover your friend has been able to read your thoughts. Upon further discussion, you discover all of your thoughts have been broadcast to the population and you've been oblivious. You begin to remember your most embarrassing and dastardly thoughts...

53.You are a private investigator hired to catch a husband's cheating wife. You try your hardest, but can't find any evidence. One day, you think you've caught her, but it's actually the husband meeting his wife. You feel like you've been sent on a wild goose chase. When you turn in the evidence, the husband tells you he was out of town that weekend...

54. A new neighbor moves into the apartment next door. To your utter dismay, spiders suddenly begin emerging from the vents. You suspect your neighbor. You decide to visit, but find something much more sinister...

55. A large corporation has mastered the practice of memory manipulation. They can add, remove, or swap memories – for a price. You had a horrible childhood. You would like to swap your memories with the memories of a child celebrity you admired as a child. Unfortunately, this child celebrity had an even more twisted childhood than yours...

56. You and your alien species finally decide to visit Earth. You land and expect either a hostile or frightened welcome. To your utter surprise, you find the people do not care. In fact, many believe you are street performers. They throw coins at you as you stroll down the street. You've never felt so disrespected in your life...

57. "What happens in Vegas, stays in Vegas," is now strictly enforced. You are allowed to enter the city and indulge in your greatest desires – no videos, no photos, no souvenirs, no memories. Write about your misadventures in a near-lawless city.

58. You live as a recluse in your parents' home. The doors and windows are sealed. Your mother delivers your meals through a doggy door. You spend your day watching the news and playing video games.

One day, the apocalypse strikes and the population dwindles. To your utter surprise, your room is the only area not affected...

59. In psychology class, you learn about suppressed memories. You ask your teacher if there's a way to find suppressed memories. Your teacher explains the process, but doesn't recommend it unless you're mentally-ill and guided by a trained psychologist. You do so anyway and find...

60. You live in a world swallowed by the oceans. Civilizations live on floating cities above the water-filled world. People are petrified of traveling due to the long trips and vicious storms. You are born with the bizarre ability to hold your breath for long periods of time – you can go hours without breathing.

61. In the near future, saving someone's life means the rescued becomes indebted to the rescuer – until death. This law is brutally enforced by governments around the world. One day, you save someone from an explosion, but soon find yourself trapped in a fire. Someone else comes to your rescue... (You can use this prompt as is, or create a never-ending loop of rescues. What would happen then?)

62. You are a prosecutor. Your next case is a vicious serial killer. When you finally meet the suspect, you find you know him and he knows you. In fact, both of you used to work together before you became a

prosecutor. The case just got much more interesting...

63. The year is 3025. There hasn't been a murder for over 1000 years. In the peaceful state, people have forgotten how to kill. When a murder suddenly occurs, a lust for blood awakens within the peaceful population. In this once-peaceful futuristic world, people revert to their old ways...

64. The world is suffering from an unprecedented crash. The poor outnumber the rich like never before. The prison system, however, continues to thrive. It may not be ideal, but prisoners have shelter and low-paying jobs – better than nothing, right? So, people begin committing crimes in order to be sent to prison. To avoid overcrowding, only the most severe offenders are sent to prison. What will you do for a warm shelter and a prison job?

65. People think you're a normal person. You try to be as normal as possible. But, they don't know your secret. Since you were a child, you've always heard a voice in your head – a voice no one else can hear. The voice of a man narrating your every move...

66. Animals around the world become inexplicably angry at humans. For example, dogs turn their backs on humans and glare at them with every command. There is one person, a sassy woman, who can actually speak to animals, but she refuses to tell you why the animals suddenly hate humans. All she says

is: "You know what you did."

67. You are a correctional officer. One day, while working at the prison, you find a prisoner you've never seen before. He's wearing the same uniform as the other inmates and he has a cell assigned to him. He acts erratically and claims to have been there for as long as he could remember. You and your peers discuss this bizarre discovery.

68. You've lived a good life. You work in construction and you've built several amazing buildings At 35-years-old, you suddenly die. You are reborn and, as you grow up, you begin to remember your past life. You end up dying again, then remember that previous life and the one before it. You find you are stuck in a cycle of never-ending reincarnation...

69. A revered psychologist, you've been asked to delve into the mind of a convicted serial killer – literally. In an attempt to comprehensively understand criminals, the government has created a device that allows you to enter the thoughts of any person. You are the first subject to enter a criminal's mind. What do you find?

70. Create a comedy by using a goofy, not-so-bright character. Here's your first scenario: Your character realizes he's not a smart guy. So, he invites people to his intervene in his life – he creates and hosts his own intervention. He's absolutely shocked to find no one showed up...

71. Your 9-year-old child has been growing stronger and stronger every day. In fact, although he's still slim and tiny, you fear he's grown stronger than you. He's also inexplicably become more skilled and agile. You suspect his elementary school is actually a government facility that trains children to become soldiers...

72. The sea pirate business has dwindled. So, pirates begin training for a new venture – air pirates. Now, pirates plan on hijacking planes straight from the sky. You can write from either perspective – someone trying to stop the pirates or an air pirate.

73. Humans have been ruled by robots for centuries. Finally, the robots decide to humor the humans and give them a single opportunity to win their freedom. The cocky robots let the human choose the challenge. The humans choose dancing. You are a robot assigned to the challenge. Unfortunately, you only know how to do the robot...

74. You are a mob boss. You're tired of the senseless killing and you're tired of the police following you around. You decide to break into the legitimate business world, so you create your own corporation. To your utter surprise, legitimate business and criminal business hardly differ. You still find yourself entrenched in violence and lawlessness...

75. You are the writer of a popular book series about

an elusive serial killer, but you've been stopped by writer's block. Soon, someone begins replicating the murders and events from your books, but the cops can't catch them. In order to stop the murder, you must complete the series...

76. In a society where everyone passionately cares about their appearance and their peers' opinions of them, the government has found a way to offset crime. If you commit a crime, the crime will be tattooed on your visible skin. You won't be allowed to cover the tattoo, either, or you'll suffer the dire consequences... What tattoos will you have? What's this society like with this new system in place?

77. You have an embarrassing secret: you can't swallow pills. Therefore, you prefer a liquid medicine. When you visit the doctor due to illness, he hands you a cup full of pills. You asks if he has it in liquid form and he sternly says, "No. Swallow the pills." Sweat starts spurting from your face like a garden sprinkler, especially when the cute nurse enters the room... What do you do?

78. While driving through a small remote town with your child, you see a child sitting at the side of the road. You stop and asks if he needs a lift. He warns: The town is filled with killer adults, don't go there. You shrug it off and visit the town anyway. You find a shocking lack of children and the adults are glaring at your kid...

79. You work long shifts through the entire night without any days off – you start to believe you are suffering from exhaustion. One day, when you arrive to work, you are told this will be your last day for a while and you can go home early – you need to use your vacation days. When you arrive home, you find someone else there. He asks, "What are you doing in my house?" You find that you've been living in the wrong home the entire time... So, where do you live?

80. It's the holiday season. You're not really a fan of Christmas, but you go with it. While at work, you realize you forgot to purchase a gift for your Secret Santa assignment. Even worse, you hear your secret Santa has purchased you an amazing gift – a gift you can't have unless you give a gift. The clock is ticking. Can you find a gift to give? Perhaps you can steal someone's gift and re-wrap it... (This is lighthearted comedy prompt. Make it silly and goofy, have a good time.)

81. You arrive at the cafe. It's nighttime and it's storming. A mysterious person has invited you for a conversation. Normally, you wouldn't talk to strangers, but this person claims to be you. He knows everything about you and he has an urgent message. As you approach the cafe, you see yourself... What is the message?

82. You have very vivid and lengthy dreams. You go to bed and have another dream. While dreaming, someone asks you, "Are you sure this isn't real? Are

you sure you didn't wake up when you went to sleep?" You wake up and find yourself in bed as normal, but you begin wondering which is your dream and which is reality...

83. The world has drastically changed. It's ruled by bandits and lawlessness. In this world, when you call the police, you have to convince the operator to send help. What makes you so special?

84. A successful anthropologist and scientist plans on using new technological discoveries to create clones of long-deceased primitive humans. He plans on placing them in theme parks and zoos to further our education and to rake in the profit. The experiment is a success and he creates a primitive human. To his utter surprise, these humans are much different than what we originally expected...

85. You are a slacker and a slob. Your brother is athletic and motivated. One day, while watching television, you are suddenly abducted. You awaken surrounded by several other abducted people – they are all fit and strong. A mysterious voice explains: You are the fittest people in your towns. You will now fight to death in our tournament. Clearly you've been mistaken for your brother. Can you survive?

86. You live alone in a small, detached home. While using the restroom, you begin to hear an indistinct voice. You trace the sound to the bathtub's water drain. You can hear bits and pieces of a sentence.

The next morning, you hear the voices again. This time, you can hear them from the sink's water drain, as well. What's happening?

87. For some inexplicable reason, people who tell lies become more attractive every time they fib. You have been considered unattractive, despite your efforts to look better. You consider lying, but you have morals. As the world population becomes gorgeous, you are faced with a decision – lie or stay ugly?

88. In order to battle the growing issue of overpopulation, the world government only allows for 41 years of life. In order to battle the issue of internet addiction, the world government forces people to pay with years of their life. How much do you cherish your life and the internet?

89. In the near-future, common roles will be reversed. You are a law-abiding citizen. Therefore, you are sent to a prison filled with other law-abiding citizens. What is this prison like? From your cell, what do you think the rest of the world is like?

90. A long-neglected genie is freed and allowed to roam the Earth for a week in a standard humanoid body. After his week vacation, he will be trapped in his bottle for eternity. However, if he can get a human to a grant him a wish, he will be allowed to roam the Earth forever.

91. Depression is running rampant – a bulk of the population are sad and tired of living. Amidst the global depression crisis, a large suicidal group declare war on those that aren't depressed. This turns into a human civil war. You are part of those that are not depressed. How do you defeat an enemy that is not afraid of dying?

92. You are an elderly man. Your wife has been nagging about your stench for years – on top of your declining health, of course. You finally visit your doctor after several years. After some tests, the doctor enters your room and says, "I don't know how to say this, but... I... I don't think you're supposed to be alive."

93. A massive, unprecedented nuclear explosion suddenly rattles a country when it wipes out an entire city in the blink of an eye. To the world's surprise, no one takes credit and there are no immediate leads. You are placed in charge to find out what happened...

94. You are a government agent part of a secret and experimental group. Your government has created a portal to Hell in order to kill the government's foes once and for all. You are being sent as the assassin. What is Hell like? Who are your targets? How do you accomplish your mission? (Perhaps your targets aren't actually in Hell...)

95. You receive an email that reads: I know who

killed your brother. But, your brother is sitting in the same room, alive and well. The next morning, you find a new email that reads: It was you. You check on your brother in the neighboring room and find he has passed...

96. You are arrested. You soon find yourself being interrogated by the police for a murder you did not commit... yet. The police have used crime-predicting technology to arrest you before your crime. Through the interrogation, explain the motives for the crime you never committed.

97. You are a very different person. Your conscience works in a different way. People can't see it, but you can. You always have a shoulder angel and a shoulder devil to help you make choices. What kind of choices will you make today?

98. A prehistoric skull is found with wounds resembling a blunt object. People suspect it is evidence of the first known homicide. You, a time detective, are sent 430,000 years back in time to solve the mystery. What happened?

99. For the past three weeks, you've suffered from terrifying nightmares. In each nightmare, you have suffered from a brutal death – stabbed, shot, car accident, ran over, poisoned, and much more. Upon some contrived research, you find someone else has died from the same death in your dreams every night.

100. You are given a mask that allows you to see people's true personalities. Some people are kind, as expected; some people are unexpectedly rude and devious. You think the mask is great, until you look into a mirror and see... (Perhaps you don't see anything? Maybe the mask is a sham? Maybe you're part of an elaborate prank?)

101. You are a police officer. One day, you receive a call from a man claiming to have your family hostage. He says he'll let them go if you can complete a list of crimes without getting caught – all in 24 hours. If you send the police to your house, your family will be killed. You reluctantly agree. The list includes burglary, robbery, battery, arson, and murder. Can you do it?

102. You're ready to pursue your dreams of becoming a writer. You sign-up for a creative writing class at your community college – your first step. You go to class, but find yourself with an unconventional teacher – a teacher that believes life experience leads to the best writing. So, this teacher asks for your ideas, then asks you to live them out before writing about it... What were your ideas? What kind of trouble do you get into, if any? (This can be an action, thriller, mystery, horror or even a comedy story.)

102 Horror Writing Prompts

For Aspiring and Experienced Writers

By Jonathan Wright

The Prompts

1. You're in the theater watching a zombie movie with your friends. After a screeching scene from the scream queen on screen, an usher stumbles into the room. His skin is pale...

2. You're driving home late one night and decide to call your buddy. However, the phone instead connects to an ongoing phone call – an argument. As the argument escalates, they mention your name...

3. You find a jar with shrunken heads in an occult shop. The clerk tells you they're real and he wants to explain the process. (Create your own process for shrinking heads.)

4. After a night of wild partying, you wake up and the reflection on the mirror is not your own.

5. You've finally completed your sleeves of tattoos. All is well until the tattoos miraculously begin to change overnight. They become more menacing and eerie every passing day...

6. A child complains to his mother about someone under his bed. The mother tells him a story about the bogeyman and shrugs it off. As she drinks her wine and listens to the radio, a news program reports an escaped pedophile with a violent record in the neighborhood...

7. Your father comes home late one night with dirt and blood under his fingernails and dirtied clothing. You are convinced he's a local serial killer. How do you stop him?

8. After a long day of class, you fall asleep on the bus on your way home. You awaken to find the bus driver is taking you to a different location...

9. Being buried alive is frightening. How about: you wake up in a pitch black area, freely levitating and spinning out of control... (like if you were in space.)

10. A man with bizarre powers enters people's dreams to kill them without a trace.

11. During a local festival on Halloween, you enter a costume contest. While on stage, you realize your competitors' costumes are much more elaborate... Almost life-life...

12. You're home alone. A man knocks on your door and claims to be your neighbor, he needs your help immediately. But, he refuses to answer any questions that would prove his identity... Can you trust him?

13. You're driving home from a concert and an emergency news report comes on. It reports that an accident has occurred on the very same highway you're driving on, but it really hasn't occurred yet... (Can you avoid your death?)

14. There is a rumor going around about a haunted clip on a website on the deep web. It's said to have the power to kill its viewer... You have to check it out...

15. You find out there is a vampire club at your local college. You decide to interview them and find they're fully immersed into their characters. Are they real vampires?

16. While you're walking home from school/work, you hear someone whisper. You turn, but find no one. After walking a few more meters, the whisper returns. Is there someone in your head? Or are you being closely followed?

17. You're obese and you're tired of it. One day, you're offered an experimental diet pill. The results are stupendous! However, even after you stop taking the pill, you continue to lose weight at an alarming pace. You feel like something is eating you from within...

18. You wake up and you're missing your right arm – it's nothing but a stub. There is no pain, though. You visit a friend and he doesn't notice anything different. You go to sleep and wake up with another missing limb, your friends don't notice... What's going on and how does it stop?

19. While grocery shopping, you find a decapitated

head near the watermelons. You shriek and report the findings, but the head vanishes.

20. You finally conjured the courage to travel by plane. You're excited for your vacation and depart successfully. All is well until you hear the staff bickering and chattering. What are they talking about? Is something wrong? You begin to panic, your imagination runs wild...

21. You have a recurring nightmare of a burning building. Someone is calling you for help, but you are reluctant. What is the source of this nightmare? (A memory? A haunting? Both?)

22. There's a haunted house in your neighborhood. For Halloween, a group of friends decide to tour the house and bring home a souvenir. The haunting, however, is real... (What souvenir do you search for? Describe the home and its history. Describe the ghost.)

23. At night, at the riverbed under the bridge, you can hear a woman crying. She's pale beyond belief and wears a torn wedding dress. (Develop the origin story for this apparition, or write about an encounter with this ghost.)

24. A game company releases a pair of goggles for augmented reality gaming and daily tasks. You receive a beta set. It's an incredibly immersive device, then you start seeing terrifying ghosts. The

company tells you it may be a glitch, but you start seeing ghosts you recognize...

25. There are always films about unseen ghosts haunting regular homes. Sometimes it's a grudged soul, sometimes it's a demon. Try writing a story where an animal haunts a house. (A dog haunts a house, write from either perspective)

26. You're driving home late through your regular residential neighborhood. Soon, you notice you're being followed. Not by a single car, but a convoy of vehicles...

27. It's prom night and you're having a great time, then you notice the chaperones have vanished. You find a drop of blood at the entrance of the auditorium and follow it to another classroom. What do you find?

28. You're spending the night alone, sitting in your living room and peacefully reading. The rain is pouring and the light is dim. From over your shoulder, you suddenly hear, "Turn the page, I'm done with this one."

29. Write a story from the perspective of a serial stalker. What are your deepest desires?

30. A new game releases for your favorite phone and tablet. You decide it's not worth your time, but soon realize people have become addicted to it. Addicted

to the point of showing symptoms similar to those of drug addiction. The addiction continues to evolve, soon you see your friends with blood dripping from their eyes...

31. Late night channel surfing leads you to a disturbing cooking program about preparing human flesh. What's the process?

32. One day, you wake up strapped to your bed and a priest is standing over you – you can hear your mother sobbing in the hall. Write from the perspective of a possessed person.

33. Write from the perspective of a vampire awakening after a hundred-year slumber. How does he adapt and what will he eat?

34. You find out your best friend, a medical student, is trying to recreate his favorite monster novel/film and he's creating a body out of stolen limbs and organs.

35. This is an oldie that really scared me as a child. You dial 666 and someone answers... What is your discussion?

36. Write from the perspective of an alien who crash lands. Unfortunately for the alien, everyone wants to kill him.

37. You find a Polaroid photograph of your deceased

grandfather. Every time you take your eyes off of it, it miraculously changes. Your grandfather looks more menacing each time, and he's getting closer to the camera...

38. You receive a frantic phone call from your best friend. He has been dead for years...

39. A serial killer takes a pill that can make him invisible. Write about his violent misadventures.

40. A man seeks companionship at night on an infamous street. He's turned away due to his shady vehicle and persona, but finds one reluctant woman who's willing to take the risk. She's not what she seems...

41. Killer dolls are common in horror. Usually a child has to survive its vicious attacks. How about a story from the doll's perspective, the doll has to survive the child's attacks? (Role reversal!)

42. You wake up in a tub full of ice. But, something hasn't been removed, something has been inserted instead... (what is it?)

43. You finally achieve your dream of becoming a kindergarten teacher. The last teacher abruptly quit. She leaves you a note that reads: Use the ruler as a long-range weapon. Tape some textbooks together to form a shield. Good luck! You soon find out these students are vicious killers looking for their next

victim. Can you survive your first day as a kindergarten teacher?

44. A thief breaks into a reclusive millionaire's home. As he silently loots the place for valuables, he finds a coffin sitting in the master bedroom. A vampire slumbers inside...

45. Not long after you move into a new house, you hear a scraping noise from the crawlspace...

46. A freelance writer falls in love with a ghost. The ghost has hidden intentions.

47. You take your significant other to lovers' lane. As you share a kiss, you hear a twig crack and the mushy grass outside. Someone is watching you...

48. You call the police after someone kicks your door open. The 911 operator doesn't seem to care and gives you dangerous advice... What's wrong with him?

49. Write from the perspective of a zombie who kills other zombies. (A zombie cannibal?)

50. A man finds himself injured and trapped in a dark room, something else is croaking nearby...

51. Create your own style of a Ouija board. Create a method to communicate with the dead.

52. You receive an email that reads: We're coming for you. What do you do?

53. A normal day in high school. Eat breakfast at the cafeteria, trudge your way through dozens of students, and finally open your locker. Wait... there's a dead body in here... Did anyone see? How did it get there?

54. You fall in love with someone you met online. He turns out to be a hideous person... inside and out... Describe this person.

55. You read the newspaper one morning and stumble upon your obituary.

56. The set of a horror film is haunted during production. What happens and why?

57. Late at night, you hear two men bickering from the baby monitor in your child's bedroom. What do you do?

58. You wake up with spiders crawling all over you... One of them gets into your mouth...

59. Write about something you think you can find in the deep web. Let your imagination run wild with the disturbing services the nearly untraceable vendors can offer you...

60. As a hardcore movie fan, the film club invites you

to watch a film at their personal theater – a vacant classroom they're allowed to use after school. You sit down with your popcorn and drink, and the movie begins... It's a snuff film.

61. A new app releases that is essentially a genie in a bottle – a genie in your phone. Rub your screen, you get three wishes. Your wishes, however, have terrifying consequences. (A modernized "Genie in a Bottle" story?)

62. You adopt a puppy. You instantly fall in love with him. Suddenly, you notice an odd surge in his growth. He's becoming more aggressive and very large...

63. Technology is growing at a rapid pace. Write a story about the horrifying consequences that can transpire. Over-reliance on computers and phones... what if it were all gone one morning? What would happen to the people? (Savages?)

64. During a visit to the zoo, the animals lose their minds and break free, viciously attacking the visitors. How do you survive?

65. You haven't slept in days, something is eating at you. Soon, you begin to hallucinate... (Write your wildest hallucinations.)

66. A janitor at an office is working late one night. Suddenly, he hears the loud clicking and clanking of

a keyboard, but he's supposed to be alone...

67. You join an anonymous video chat and find yourself talking to a black screen – you can only hear his raspy voice. It's all fun and games until he mentions your name... the name you never told him. (How does he know?)

68. You find a music box during a yard sale. One night, while you're resting in bed, you decide to play it. Suddenly, you hear loud thumps surrounding your bed... (Are you making the spirits dance?)

69. Serial killers compete for the highest kill count in Los Angeles.

70. You're working late one night at a restaurant. A man walks in with blood trickling down his ear and torn clothing. The man asks, "Do you serve brains?"

71. Write from the perspective of a female stalker. We have enough male antagonists, what would a female stalker do?

72. The Hook is a classic urban legend about a killer with a hook for a hand. What if he really existed today? How would he stalk and execute his victims? (Modernize an urban legend.)

73. Write from the perspective of a ghost haunting a house? Why do you haunt the home? What would you do if you were invisible?

74. Your attic harbors sinister secrets... What's hiding up there?

75. You find your grandfather's childhood journal. He was experiencing the same haunting as you...

76. A comic book artist finds his horrifying creations are coming to life, so he draws creatures with good personalities to fight them off. (Horror/action hybrid story?)

77. A killer strain of the flu is killing off the population. How do you survive?

78. A demon offers you a lucrative wish and promises it won't backfire. In order to get the wish, however, you must kill the person you care about most... Yourself...

79. Your plane crash lands on an uncharted island. The tribes eat people who are different. How far will you go to adapt? (Cannibalism?)

80. You wake up at night, but find you can't move. You panic, but try to convince yourself it's a nightmare. Before you can slumber again, you hear people shuffling inside your room and whispering indistinctly... (Sleep paralysis? Kidnapping? Abduction? Take it anywhere!)

81. You're a journalist searching for the best meal in

town. You hear of a lucrative club offering the rarest foreign steak. When you show up, you find a club of reclusive millionaires awaiting their meal – what is it?

82. In your small town, you find that there really is a troll under the bridge. This troll is hungry for humans. (What does this troll look like? How do you get past him?)

83. You're on a cruise. Everything is swell. Suddenly, a warning goes out: the boat is sinking. The worst part: you don't know how to swim! (True-to-life horror.)

84. A death row inmate awaiting his execution finds his victims haunting his prison cell. The ghosts are hateful and will use anything in the cell to kill him... Can the death row inmate survive the onslaught?

85. On Halloween, you and your friends egg the wrong house...

86. Write from the perspective of a security camera that captures a brutal slaying from a notorious serial killer. The camera constantly sways, so it only catches bits and pieces of the crime. (Create a horrifying puzzle with your words.)

87. Describe the torture room of a sadistic maniac. After that, describe his home. Where does that vicious killer sleep?

88. What would you do if you were a werewolf?

89. A man commits suicide by cutting his wrists, but wakes up the next morning – he has scars on his wrists from the attempted suicide. Shrugging it off, he decides to hang himself, but still wakes up the next morning – there are bruises on his neck. Why can't he die?

90. You're invited to record an actual exorcism. Break away from the common cliches, no more bone-popping or crawling on walls; what would your demon do?

91. While surfing the web, you find a website about live torture. People can bid to torture the unwilling participants. You notice your high school bully is up next in the torture queue. Do you report the site to the police? Or do you participate in the torture from the comfort of your home?

92. You break into a long-abandoned high school with your friends. As you prepare an indoor bonfire in the large auditorium, you're attacked by zombie hobos.

93. A witch claims to have the ability to send anyone to hell for up to 2 hours. You're curious and decide to take her up on that offer. What if she actually sends you to hell? What is your definition of hell?

94. You visit a website that can predict your death – method and date. It says you'll die today. (What does the website look like? What's the method?)

95. You awaken and find yourself free-falling – quickly plummeting to Earth without a parachute. What happened?

96. You are dreaming about paradise. You wake up in the forest. A striking pain in your hand, you drop your knife. A dead body is at your feet. What did you do?

97. You find human hair in your bowl of beef stew at a new restaurant. The waiters ignore you. You take your bowl and step into the kitchen where you make a horrendous discovery...

98. During your travels in Japan, you purchase a camera that supposedly allows you to capture spirits. It works...

99. There aren't enough horror stories about animals and creatures. How about a story about a legendary beast, the hellhound...

100. You peek through the crack of your closet door. Someone has entered your home and he has a large knife. How do you escape?

101. You visit Japan's infamous suicide forest, Aokigahara. How do you feel? (Can you feel the lost

spirits watching you?)

102. You finally decide to write a collection of scary short stories. The night before your book is set to release, the nightmares you've created invade your home...

102 Horror Writing Prompts Vol. 2

For Aspiring and Experienced Writers

By Jonathan Wright

The Prompts

1. You are a priest. After extensive research, you believe your nation's leader is possessed by the Devil. You present your findings to the higher-ups and the authorities, but people shrug it off and call you crazy. You take matters into your own hands and decide to exorcise your nation's leader. How do you do it?

2. You are a scientist hired by the government to research a new and rapidly-spreading disease – a sexually-transmitted disease that causes people to turn into vicious zombies. While you research, you are in the safety of a military bunker. From within the bunker, you watch the zombie outbreak spread as people follow their lust. What do you see? Can you stop it from spreading?

3. You are a lonely college student. You show up to your community college for another day of dreadful class. But, wait, something is off. The other students seem to be stuck on their phones. Like zombies, the student body is drawn to a popular free-to-play mobile game. Soon, the world starts to crash around you as the addiction spreads...

4. During your child's birthday party, your child withdraws into his room. You shrug it off as normal for an introverted kid. The party clown tries to follow him, you think that's strange. He's eager to enter your child's bedroom, he even peeks through

the window. You cancel the party and send the clown home. The following day, the clown shows up at your door and says he urgently needs to speak to your child. He says, "There's someone hiding in your child's closet…" (This is practically an entire story, but it's an effective prompt to practice your storytelling and descriptive writing. Practice creating suspense and mystery.)

5. You drink an elixir that summons a genie. The genie offers you three wishes, no-strings-attached. However, in order to redeem your wishes, you must deliver the souls of three family members. Your mom, your dad, your sister, and your brother are home. What do you do? Do you kill your family and trust the genie? Maybe you can wish them back to life…

6. You are an expert dog-trainer. You are called to an eerie house at the bad side of town. A peculiar woman answers the door, she tells you she's a witch and she needs a trainer for her pet. You laugh it off – perhaps she's crazy, but she's already paid. You go to the backyard and find a hellhound waiting for you. Can you train this mystical creature?

7. To receive feedback before their debut, a video game company sends you a complimentary virtual-reality headset. The experience is unbelievable, you feel like you've entered a new world. Then, you start seeing ghosts. You shrug it off as a glitch, but then you recognize the ghosts as people from your past…

8. On the eve of his execution, a man on death row is confronted by his many victims. The ghosts, however, are not physically malicious. Instead, these ghosts recount their stories and try to convince the death row inmate to commit suicide before his execution.

9. A psychopath with homicidal urges posts an ad online: Are you suicidal? Let me kill you! To his utter surprise, the suicidal residents of his small town respond to his message by the dozens. To their utter shock, they won't die so easily... They'll have to endure his agonizing torture.

10. You are a stalker. One day, you plant cameras in the home of your unrequited love. You watch her everyday, like if you were watching regular television. One day, you notice someone else is breaking into her home and she's in trouble. What do you do? (This writing prompt is for more of a "creepy" horror story. Far less traditional, but you can conjure some goosebumps with some eerie descriptions.)

11. A lonesome writer finds passion in his writing. However, his passion goes too far when he falls in love with a tormented character he created. A character of the opposite gender with a striking resemblance. He finds comfort and solace in knowing she had endured similar pain. One morning, he wakes up and his creation is in bed with

him...

12. You are a depressed person. You are tired with life, you are tired of the disappointment and loneliness. One night, you contemplate suicide. Before you can pull the trigger of your firearm, you are confronted by your doppelganger. The doppelganger says, "We need to talk. It is urgent."

13. A young and devious teenager enters an anonymous video chat website. He sees the regularly-scheduled nudity, particularly male nudity, but then stumbles upon a person restrained to a chair. From the safety of his home, he witnesses the person's torture. Despite the urge to report his findings, he's drawn to the torture and watches more...

14. On Halloween, you and your friends go on a cross-country trip to find the most terrifying haunted houses. Unfortunately, everything seems like child's play – jump-scares and obvious costumes. You decide to visit an extreme underground horror house. This house is comprised of five rooms of torture. You must witness each room to escape or you'll be a replacement in one of the rooms...

15. You have always been a peculiar person. Throughout high school, whenever you were asked to drink, you passed up on the opportunity. People would tease you for abiding by the laws of underage

drinking, but you wouldn't let the peer pressure get to you. You know, if you drink too much, you'll start seeing ghosts...

16. After another failed date, a man in an alley offers to remedy your pain and fulfill your greatest desires. Skeptical at first, you're sold when the man reveals how much he knows about you. He leads you to a gray storage van. Within the van, your previous but failed love interests are gagged and blindfolded. For a special price, you can do anything you want to them... Anything.

17. Two drug addicts decide to experiment with a gnarly Russian drug. A cheap-but-effective drug that can eat you from the inside if it's abused. The pair fall unconscious, then awaken to find themselves literally falling apart. Their skin is black and scaly, their ears and noses are falling from their faces, and so on. They never expected the drug to be so effective!

18. Tired of being a loser, a young man creates a time machine and concocts a devious plan to save his future. In order to do so, however, he'll have to kill himself in the past and replace himself. His plans immediately fall apart and the man decides to become a time-traveling serial killer instead...

19. A journalist is secretly invited to interview a notorious serial killer at a desolate location. Upon arrival, the journalist is knocked unconscious. The

journalist awakens restrained to a chair and the serial killer says, "It's my turn to interview you." The catch: every wrong answer results in insufferable pain.

20. One day, you awaken to find an inexplicable peephole in your bedroom. The peephole leads to your neighbor's bedroom – your unrequited love's bedroom. You peek through and watch her as she is oblivious of the hole. One day, while peeping, you see yourself enter her bedroom and kill her. A doppelganger?

21. You awaken due to a blaring car horn. You find yourself in the trunk of a vehicle. You begin to panic, but you don't shout. You hear the faint voice of men talking in the vehicle. With very few options, you recompose yourself and try to make out their conversation. What's going on? Where are they taking you?

22. You are a teenager. You are saddened to hear your grandfather is on his deathbed. You visit your grandfather on his deathbed and he begins to recount his life. He confesses to heinous crimes as a notorious serial killer. You are shocked. You are more shocked to hear he wants you to continue in his tradition.

23. You live a seemingly regular life as a high school student. One morning, on your social media account, you receive a message from a young man that goes

to your school. You are utterly shocked – this student died over six months ago due to bullying. The message reads: Help me exact my vengeance or I'll haunt you until death. Do you follow along? Or is this another devious prank from the school bullies?

24. A lonely autopsy technician finds himself drawn to the corpse of a gorgeous young woman. He can't explain his feelings, but he inexplicably adores the woman. Consequently, he'll go to any length to protect the deceased woman from an internal examination... Any length. (This is another creepy prompt. Try creating dialogue between the autopsy technician and the corpse. Create a sense of hopeless romance between the pair.)

25. Amidst a zombie apocalypse, a clueless corporation believes they can profit off the zombies. They believe they can create a product the zombies will buy. The corporation decides on a new chain of fast food restaurants. You are in charge of leading the marketing team for this strange project that is bound to fail... or is it?

26. You are convinced you're possessed by a demon or the Devil. You ask your doctors about the possibility – they believe it may be a mental illness. You ask your priest – he believes you should see a doctor. Without much help from anyone, you decide to exorcise the demon yourself. How do you do it? Can you succeed?

27. While digging through a yard sale, you are drawn to a peculiar cellphone. A large and bulky cellphone. You purchase it believing it'll be a perfect gag. When you use it, you find you can communicate with the dead. You decide to make a buck off your discovery and allow people to contact the dead for a price... You soon find the dead do not like to be disturbed.

28. While late-night channel surfing, you stumble upon a strange game show seemingly hosted from Hell. The rules: three participants will be tortured until death; the audience will vote on the torture method and must stay for the entire show; if an audience member quits, they'll replace one of the participants. You decide to stick around and vote. You are shocked to see your mother is one of the participants to be tortured... Can you endure the show?

29. You are a struggling actor. You think you deserve better. You know you deserve better. So, you seize the opportunity to become famous overnight. You participate in a satanic ritual... (Some plot point ideas: Describe your humble or not-so-humble beginnings; describe the satanic ritual in vivid detail; describe the aftermath; etc.)

30. You live alone in a small apartment. Although you are occasionally lonely, you live a comfortable life. One night, as your are preparing for bed, someone knocks on your bedroom door. You are petrified and you hide under the covers like a child.

The door cracks open and a man's voice asks, "Are you sleeping?" Before you can answer, you awaken the following morning. This is the start of a never-ending cycle... What is happening?

31. Write from the perspective of a maniacal but skilled surgeon. You hate people, you've lost hope in humanity. But, you love animals. So, you rationalize: if you can combine your favorite animals with the humans you despise most, you can create a new, lovable species. So, doctor, what kind of insane creature will you create?

32. You are a child. Your mother loves you, despite some of your bad behavior. One night, after being suspended from school, your mom tucks you into bed and sings you a lullaby. The lullaby threatens to kill you... (This is more of a psychological horror prompt. This will also give you the opportunity to practice writing rhythmic tones, such as a creepy lullaby.)

33. You are a concerned parent. After hearing rumors of a pedophile nurse at your child's school, you decide to investigate more. You catch the nurse sucking on the knee of a child after a playground accident. You aren't convinced he's a pervert, though, you think he's a vampire instead... And you just might be correct.

34. For your college anthropology class, you and your group decide to investigate ancient linguistics.

You find a book with a black cover in your library. The book tells of an ancient creature that stalks its prey and kills them if it's spotted. At the library, you accidentally summon the creature. You find that you can't look over your shoulder, or it'll kill you...

35. An ambitious archaeologist leads a gullible team of amateurs into a deep cavern. Unfortunately, you become trapped as the rocks shift and close your only opening. Although everyone is fine, the archaeologist immediately begins to hallucinate. He believes he's dug into Hell and the Devil wants him to kill his team...

36. You are a loving and caring person. You decide to participate in humanitarian work in a third-world country. You are excited to help and gain life experience. When you arrive, you are utterly shocked to find the poor and starving people have resorted to eating each to survive. (This one is a little raw and it can hit home for some, but true-to-life horrors are very effective.)

37. After a long business trip, you decide to stay at a roadside motel in the desert. All is well until you hear a fight erupt in the room next door. The commotion is loud and the wall trembles from the presumed fight. You place your ear to the wall and listen to the argument... What do you hear?

38. You are the regular babysitter for your neighbor's child. You arrive ready for duty at the

regular time, but you find the parents have already departed. You take care of the child, but the parents never arrive. You call them and ask when they'll be home and you joke about overtime. They ask why you're in their house since they're mourning the death of their child the weekend prior. Who are you babysitting?

39. While playing baseball, the ball rolls into a storm drain. The kids peer and reach inside to no avail. Before departing, they hear a voice from the sewer. The voice convinces the kids to slaughter their parents...

40. When he consumes a psychedelic mushroom, a man finds that ghosts are real and they live in our dimension – some peacefully and some maliciously. On account of his recreational drug use, people don't believe him. Can you convince society that your shrooms can help the people reconnect with the dead? Or are you just tripping?

41. You've believed you are a seemingly regular person your entire life. You were destined for boredom. One day, you find a note on your front door: "We want you, Father. Come to us." Although initially afraid you've had a child, you find you are being relentlessly pursued by a cult that believes you are the reincarnation of Satan.

42. Your sweet and loving grandmother has come to visit. All is well until the neighborhood kids start to

disappear. Your imagination begins to run wild – grandma or coincidence? After the sudden string of disappearances, you believe your grandmother is kidnapping the neighborhood kids and cooking them for your favorite "chewy" cookies.

43. A conniving child on Christmas Eve plans to stay up and catch his father placing the gifts under the Christmas tree. He refuses to believe Santa Claus is real. To his utter surprise, he finds Santa has actually arrived. Unfortunately, this Santa is a demon and he's here to punish the naughty...

44. A young teenager wrecks havoc across his neighborhood. When his reign of terror is finally stopped, he believes he'll be sent to juvenile hall. Instead, the judge sends him to a special camp. A camp with extreme methods of fixing deviant behavior. (This may work more effectively as a true-to-life horror story. Create something eerie and disturbing.)

45. You are a journalist. You need a scoop or your career will be over before it begins. You decide to join and infiltrate a Satan-worshiping cult. To your utter surprise, the cult turns you into a member and you like your position – you like the cult members and you agree with their beliefs. So, you decide to spread Satan's word through your journalism.

46. You are a dirty cop. You rose through the rankings thanks to your high arrest and conviction

rates. However, one night, after using excessive force to kill someone, you find yourself haunted by everyone you've framed... The only way to alleviate your haunting: confess.

47. You are a young teenager. You and your friends decide to roam the sewers in search of treasure and riches. You figure at least you'll find a sewer alligator and capture some great pictures. Instead, you find a demonic creature lurking in the sewers. To your benefit, the creature is blind and can't seem to find an exit...

48. You awaken to pure darkness. You can't remember your name. You can't remember the night prior. In fact, you can't remember anything. You can, however, hear someone's voice. You rationalize, you are a voice in a man's head. Can you convince him to help you escape? Or are you the root of a more severe mental issue?

49. Write from the perspective of an ambitious, up-and-coming news anchor. From the safety of your television studio, you are reporting on a national zombie outbreak — from the origin of the outbreak. You can't leave your position, either, you are responsible for documenting and reporting the outbreak to the concerned citizens... (This zombie prompt can go anywhere. Perhaps, your news anchor feels squeamish from the violent footage that airs. Perhaps, you have to report dangers occurring near your family and you're helpless. Experiment

with this secluded environment.)

50. You and your friends travel to Mexico to score cheap drugs and meet beautiful women. The experience is initially wonderful for your group of deviants. However, by nighttime, you are kidnapped by a mysterious group. You believe it's a cartel seeking a hefty ransom, but you soon witness a bizarre sacrifice and find religious symbols scattered throughout their compound... A satanic cult?

51. You wake up with sharp wounds on your body, like if you've been stabbed by a needle. You shrug it off as an insect bite. You wake up the next morning with a bruised eye and a broken arm – maybe you slept in the wrong position? As the inexplicable wounds pile up, you begin to suspect you are a victim of a voodoo doll. Who's responsible? Can you stop it?

52. A serial killer uses an anonymous web chat to broadcast his murders. To his utter surprise, he becomes famous. Even more shocking: people start to copy him in order to attain the same fame. With everyone joining his business, the serial killer suddenly finds himself at odds with his initial lust for blood...

53. You're a ghost causing havoc. You scare people for fun, you disorganize people's apartments, and you love making the doors squeak. While planning a

new prank, you abruptly die. To your surprise, you find there is an afterlife to the afterlife – an after-afterlife!

54. You are an extravagant and hardworking businessman. You are constantly traveling. One day, while traveling abroad to an important business meeting, you fear the plane is going to wrong way. As your flight approaches a storm, your plane begins to tremble irrepressibly. You fear you are either crashing or entering a new dimension...

55. You are a naive high school student and a hardcore horror fan who has seen one too many slashers. When your fellow classmates begin showing up dead and you find a teacher with blood on his tie, you begin to suspect the faculty is responsible... You might be correct...

56. You are a claustrophobic man. You awaken inside a very tight coffin without any recollection of the past. You have a lighter, some flammable fluid, and a box cutter. The thoughts run through your mind, but you're always led to suicidal thoughts. Can you escape and survive?

57. While riding your subway train back home from school, the train suddenly stalls. The train feels hotter than before and you can see smoke approaching from the darkness. You begin hearing whispers and whimpers in the tunnel. Something is approaching your train...

58. You are studying late one night. You hear a crash from the attic. You decide to investigate. When you enter the attic, you find a large body mirror towards the center of the storage room. As you stare at the mirror, your reflection begins to inexplicably swirl. You touch the reflection on the mirror and the reflection ripples like a puddle... A portal?

59. You are a computer specialist. You love developing apps and hacking servers. One day, you find a website that supposedly allows you to talk to ghosts through your webcam. It catches your attention because it always delivers a unique and creepy experience. You decide to hack the site, but unwittingly unleash the ghosts trapped in the website... (This is a technology-horror prompt.)

60. While watching an opera, you begin to see eerie silhouettes behind the female performer. Suddenly, the woman glares at you and only you. She hits a high note and the other patrons suddenly suffer from spontaneous combustion – the audience members are burned alive. You are the only survivor of this mysterious massacre...

61. During a cold night, you are approached by a person claiming to be a vampire. This person is exactly what you've wanted in your love life, the person is inexplicably attractive. Consequently, this person convinces you to siphon the blood of unwitting people as they sleep...

62. You are a reporter. While reporting from a march against drugs, the group is ferociously attacked by people with bloodshot eyes and bulging veins. You learn that these people have used a home-made drug called Rampage, and it causes the user to become psychotic...

63. Write from the perspective of a soldier in a private military. You and a group of carefully selected elite soldiers are being shipped to a secluded location in Mexico to help the locals fight. You suspect you are fighting the cartel. In a sense, you are correct. Except, these cartel members are undead...

64. You cough and groan as you spiral into consciousness – literally. You find yourself in a dark room, your body is flinging around, like if you're hanging from a rope. You find you are restrained by silky filaments. As you try to escape, you see the silhouette of a spider approaching... It's much larger than any insect you've ever seen.

65. Write from your everyday perspective. You wake up one morning and find something is different. You stagger into the restroom and find your skin is peeling. Your skin continues to peel until you finally start seeing blood, then bone...

66. You are a ghost hunter. You enter an old manor with your ghost hunting crew in hopes of finding

real ghosts. While exploring, you find a hidden laboratory behind a large bookcase in the manor's library. The laboratory is filled with journals of past experiments. Soon, you and your crew begin to experience abnormal events and you find yourselves trapped in the home. (Create an alternative explanation for the presumed haunting. Perhaps an experiment has caused the manor's owner to become invisible?)

67. You wake up and find you've lost all feeling to your right forearm and hand. To your utter surprise, your right arm begins to move on its own – you can't control its actions, no matter how hard you try. For some inexplicable reason, your arm has a mind of its own and it's becoming more malicious every day... (Create an explanation for the inexplicable. Make your arm the antagonist. This can be a Science-Fiction/Horror prompt, or something more psychological.)

68. You're tired of your dull life. You decide to quit school and pursue your dreams – you want to become a certified clown. You visit a training camp and start pursuing your goals, you're excited. The excitement dwindles when you realize this camp actually trains aspiring clowns to be menacing and creepy. Even worse, this school tends to award those clowns for murder...

69. In our modern world, werewolves are real. The government has tried to kill them, but they are too

powerful and cunning. During full moons, you and your family must fortify your home to survive. Describe your fortified home and the thoughts running through your mind. (Of course, this prompt can be expanded. Perhaps a werewolf breaks through your barriers?)

70. You are a hard-boiled detective. You are on the trail of a serial killer. After finding a batch of severely mutilated bodies, you notice they look similar to a comic you've read. Upon further contemplation, you realize you look like a character in that comic...

71. While visiting your mother, you find an old photo book. While looking through the pictures, you notice something peculiar. There is always an eerie man standing in the background of your photos. You try to shrug it off, but then you look through the photos in your cellphone – the man is still there...

72. Your mother sends you to your hoarder grandmother's home to help her clean up the mess cluttering the house. As you arrive, you immediately notice the putrid stench surrounding the home. As you enter the home, the stench becomes stronger and you find your grandmother is absent. You find there are piles of trash larger than your body littering the home. As you begin cleaning, you find a decomposing hand protruding from the trash...

73. After an exhaustive month of work, you decide to depart and finally go on your dream vacation. While

flying abroad for your first time, you begin to believe there are ghosts on the plane. You see people moving about on the plane, but they continuously leave and never reappear. You see a man with a conniving grin walk through another person and towards the cockpit...

74. You are a researcher leading a group deep into sea to investigate. The deeper you descend, the more you fear for the safety of your crew. You begin to fear they may hallucinate and there won't be a way out. Then, you see a scaly, menacing creature you've never seen before swim by your submarine... Perhaps you're hallucinating?

75. Solitary confinement is a psychological exercise for some inmates. You are a prisoner and you are sent to solitary confinement after a violent fight. In your small cell, you feel the walls start to close in on you. You hear an irritable whisper from beyond your cell. You see something move in the shadows. Is someone else with you?

76. You are a demon. You've been given a pass to Earth. You enter the Earth realm as an incorporeal spirit. Like most demons on vacation, you've decided to possess a child and have some fun. (Write from the perspective of a demon in a boy's body. You can use this horror prompt to poke fun at common possession clichés.)

77. You find extraterrestrials exist. You find this

alien species has been abducting humans and creating clones of them. These clones are sent to a new planet resembling Earth and the clones are examined by the aliens. You believe you are a clone.

78. While searching for a box of tapes to sell, you find a roll of film in the attic. You watch the film to your utter dismay. The film depicts the disturbing murder of your family at your hands and you suddenly feel a lust for blood... Can you stop the premonition?

79. You are a vicious assassin. You're an expert in the field and a notorious legend. One day, you find your past victims have come back to life. The only way to get rid of them for good is to kill them again using the same method of their original death. With such a high body count, let's hope you can put a death to the face. (This works more as a horror-action prompt.)

80. After a hard day, you stroll down the beach at dusk. The sunset is beautiful. You see something peculiar on the coast, though. A creature you can't identify jumping in-and-out of the water. The creature soon crashes onto the shore. Your heart races as you suspect it may be a mermaid – the love you have been waiting for is right over the horizon. When you approach the creature, it's much more horrendous than you imagined... (Create a horrifying mermaid. What happens next? Kick it back into shore or bring it home?)

81. You and your wife live in a secluded cabin in the woods. Afters years of trying and failing, you decide to adopt a child. You figure you can provide the child with love, support, and education from the safety of your home. After raising your child for two years, you realize the child has been dead for a decade...

82. While instant messaging with your friends, you are invited to chat by someone you don't initially know. You humor the person and chat with him. To your utter surprise, he knows everything about your childhood – things he couldn't possibly know. He reveals that he is your father... but your father died when you were a child...

83. You are a surgeon working the emergency room at the local hospital. Through your work, you've seen the most horrible and gruesome accidents. One night, a family rush their son into the emergency room. He's sick, groaning as he foams from the mouth. As you try to find the cause, you begin to suspect he's a zombie... Or, maybe you're just exhausted...

84. You are a young and timid college student living alone off-campus in a small studio apartment. Every night as you try to sleep, you feel a pair of eyes piercing into you – menacingly staring at you. One night, you believe you see someone watching you from the window in your bedroom. (Write from the perspective of someone being stalked. A true-to-life

horror prompt.)

85. Write from the perspective of a frail ghost. You live in a desolate home in the woods far from civilization. You soon find your home invaded by ghost hunters. You keep quiet and hope they'll leave, but they continuously pretend to "feel" your presence. These humans are beginning to frighten and bother you. This is a reverse haunting.

86. You and your friends download a Ouija Board app for your tablet computer. You don't care for the rules and your group disrespects a ghost – it's not real, anyway, right? Soon, you find you've summoned a serial killer's ghost – a serial killer who stalked his victim's through social media. Now, this apparition can travel through electronic devices... (A cliché Ouija board prompt converted into a technology horror prompt. Should be interesting.)

87. You are an art house filmmaker seeking to create a visually-stimulating and artful ghost film. You decide to try and capture real ghosts. You follow the classic formula – if a person dies in a fit of rage, they become a ghost. So, you annoy your employees until they're angry, then kill them on set. You may be psychotic, but you just might have the most realistic ghost film ever made...

88. You have been working on your new book for far too long. You've spent countless hours writing, rewriting, editing, and so on. You decide to go on

vacation to a cheap island resort. When you land, you find the residents live in perfect harmony with terrifying but peaceful ghosts. (This can be a serious horror prompt, but it may work more effectively as a fun and goofy horror prompt.)

89. A doctor begins conducting bizarre experiments to cure his insane patients. He performs unsafe surgeries on their brains, he locks them in dark rooms for days, he feeds them too much or too little. This doctor just might be the most insane of them all. (This prompt doesn't have to be gratuitous. In fact, this exercise will help in practicing restraint while creating disturbing situations.)

90. Your home has been burglarized several times. You've been robbed twice in the last two months. You purchase and train a dog to kill. Your home is safer until your dog suddenly runs away. Not before long, the news begins covering a psychopathic dog killing everyone on the block like a serial killer... and you're responsible.

91. You decide to pursue a career in cooking. You sign-up for a special culinary course that will help you prepare the finest meats. You arrive at the suspiciously secluded classroom and find yourself learning how to prepare human flesh for consumption. The other students are enthralled and there are no refunds...

92. You and your significant other are thrill hunters.

After some debate, you decide to purchase a supposedly haunted home – it's cheap and it should be thrilling. The home, however, begins to take a toll on your sanity and you find yourself despising your lover... If she even exists...

93. You work at a retirement home. You've met some peculiar residents, but it has mostly been calm work. One day, a mysterious elderly man begins to babble about murders he claims to have committed. You search the murders and find he's very accurate with the details. Is he telling the truth? Or is he mentally ill?

94. You are given the opportunity to win $10 million dollars. In order to do so, you must stick your hand in a case of syringes and find a thin, red needle in under three minutes... Hopefully you don't ooze too much blood!

95. One day, you begin receiving disturbing phone calls. A man croaking and grunting as he struggles to speak. You try to shrug it off to no avail – the man keeps calling. Suddenly, the man claims he's going to kill you. You track the phone call, only to find it's coming from your phone... How is this possible? Who is the mysterious man?

96. You purchase an antique mirror from a mysterious seller on a classified advertisement website. He claims the mirror has caused him and the previous owners nothing but misfortune. When

it arrives, you begin to experience terrifying nightmares. You shatter the mirror, but it always returns in its original form... (Create a terrifying origin for the haunted mirror.)

97. You are a drug mule for a powerful drug cartel. Your bosses have inserted a very special package into your rectum and they're sending you to Mexico. While crossing the border, you feel the package shatter and something begins crawling in your body...

98. You are a backpacking serial killer traveling through foreign countries and killing other naive backpackers. One day, while stalking your next victim, you witness something eerily familiar. Said victim is also stalking a backpacker. You find he's also in the same business... Will you join forces to create a sinister duo? Or will you clash for the highest kill-count?

99. You are awakened by a splash. You find yourself on a row boat in the middle of a body of water and surrounded by a dense, impenetrable fog. You look towards the water – you can still see the small waves and ripples from the splash. What's down there?

100. You purchase a set of walkie-talkies to play with your son. One day, you find your son talking to someone. You initially believe he might have caught some interference or he might have found someone's radio frequency, but the toy radio only

has a few meters in range. Is someone else in the home?

101. You are a private investigator. You are hired by a worried woman to find her missing husband. You have his picture and background information. You are led to a bar, which leads you to a ventriloquist. This ventriloquist has an eerily familiar puppet... It almost looks human.

102. You are a successful writer. You've published some critically-acclaimed books and you're adored by your fans. One day, you receive a scathing review from an angry customer. Your ego takes a major blow. You decide to practice black magic and create a voodoo doll of those who leave negative reviews. Your vengeance is just getting started.

102 SciFi and Fantasy Writing Prompts

For Aspiring and Experienced Writers

By Jonathan Wright

The Prompts

1. While working in your basement laboratory, you create a device that allows interdimensional travel. While conducting the first test, you find the device works. From your dimension, you can see into the other dimension. Consequently, you see another version of yourself, who also create an interdimensional traveling device. You agree to take a tour of his world as it seems to be an exact replica, but you soon find it is radically and dangerously different...

2. Our world is under a police state. Everyone is being monitored by devices implanted into their heads – a device that can predict and judge future crimes. Depending on the severity of their criminal thoughts and probability, the device will either deduct money from their bank accounts, knock them unconscious and send them to prison, or self-destruct causing the citizen's head to explode.

3. You are the King of the land. You've ruled with an iron fist and you plan to continue your dominance by invading the neighboring kingdoms. But, alas, you've fallen terminally ill. Your adviser tells you of a nearby forest that harbors a secreting healing well – in order for it to work, the sick must traverse the eerie forest on their own... (This can work as a simple adventure or it can be converted into a coming-of-age tale.)

4. You are an expertly-skilled detective – the best in your town. One day, you are abducted and brought to an abandoned apartment building. Your captors explain: they need you to travel back in time and find a misbehaving perp who may be changing significant events in history... (This time travel prompt is an excellent exercise in creativity. You can bend the rules and create amazing twists. For example, perhaps the perp you are after is responsible for your skills – you'd be no one without him. Experiment with it.)

5. In the near future, a deadly disease will cause people to turn into powerful werewolves. The government has assigned you to lead a team of expertly-trained soldiers to hunt these powerful beasts. As the hunt continues, you begin to suspect someone on your team has been infected...

6. A computer specialist attempts to hack into a secure server suspected of harboring invaluable information and assets. During the process, he finds photographs and reports of aliens at a nearby military base. He soon finds he's hacked into a government server and aliens are real... What do you do with this information? Are you safe?

7. There has been a recent increase in murders in a nearby forest. The government officials blame animal attacks, but the remains are far too mangled to be from a woodland animal. You and some friends decide to investigate, you enter the forest and soon

realize you are not alone. There are soldiers and cops wandering the forest, too. Even worse, you find an army of Orcs have somehow entered our modern world...

8. Despite strong social norms and ethics, a lonely scientist creates an android lover. He fears he'll be stigmatized and ridiculed by society and his peers, but he can't handle the overwhelming loneliness. When he struts his android companion through town, he experiences the unforeseeable consequences of science – the other men in town have fallen in love with his android...

9. You awaken sitting next to a hospital bed. Your unconscious body is resting on said bed. You overhear a conversation: you were in a car accident, you are in a coma. In disbelief, you start to break everything in the room. Your family and hospital staff see your mayhem, but they can't see you – they think the hospital is haunted. You realize you are free to interact with anything without consequence... No one will ever know it was you. You're in a coma, after all...

10. After years of work, a scientist creates a cure for aids. The scientist reaps the rewards, but soon finds his cure has caused the disease to become airborne... (Write from the perspective of the scientist. The world is crashing because of your invention, despite your good deeds. What was the world like? What is it now? How does the scientist feel?)

11. A man struggling to support his family decides to commit as many robberies as possible – he's willing to lose his life to death or prison as long as his family receives some financial support. He decides to rob an occult shop, but finds the staff aren't solely human... They are humans, elves, and wizards from another dimension. They offer you gold in exchange for a little adventure...

12. An amateur scientist (i.e. basement scientist) finds a way to clone animals. He figures it will be good for creating a surplus of food, he feels like a genius who has saved the world from starvation. However, the animals he clones end up having greater intelligence and aggressive behavior...

13. As an aspiring athlete, you aim to be the very best. Unfortunately, you haven't reached that goal. In fact, it's out of your reach. One day, a mysterious man loitering near the locker room offers you an experimental drug – an untraceable steroid that will give you immeasurable strength... (Create some unintended consequences.)

14. The last of the human species have used dragon scales to create powerful armor and weapons. Soon, they find the dragon population dwindling and an evil army is approaching quickly. You, a young and naive human, along with your elder brother, are sent to find the elusive Dragon King before the army arrives... (Why are you searching for the Dragon

King? What is the Dragon King? An all-powerful dragon? A human who can tame dragons?)

15. While browsing your television after midnight, you find an eerie channel filled with static – it's inexplicably mesmerizing. As you continue watching, the picture becomes clear and reveals a man slumped forward in a chair. He suddenly awakens and invites you into his realm. Miraculously, you enter the television and find... (Create a world within the television. This is more of a horror/fantasy prompt, but feel free to experiment.)

16. Write from the perspective of an android president. In a sense, humans have been enslaved and robots live the luxurious life. For example, in the future, fast food restaurants only hire humans for cheap labor and only serve robots. As president, you see an uprising in terrorist attacks and must act... Can you stop the human uprising? (This is a role reversal prompt that can help you create a unique world by simply reversing roles. A futuristic world where humans, instead of robots, make the world spin.)

17. You're a self-righteous and aggressively judgmental person. You are pretentious and narcissistic. One day, while judging a man's reckless driving, you are killed in a car accident. To your surprise, the Grim Reaper invites you to become his assistant...

18. In the near future, scientists discover a way to temporarily combat death with a respawning mechanism – essentially, everyone on the planet is given nine lives. Imagine the beauty and mayhem of life... What would you do with nine lives?

19. Earth begins intercepting bizarre audio messages and signals in space. The language has never been heard before. The government suspects extraterrestrials, they also fear the aliens may have malicious intentions. You are given the assignment: decrypt the messages and decide if it's threatening... The planet's safety is in your hands. (Try developing a new language. This is also a great prompt for practicing your writing in suspense.)

20. In the near future, an amusement park will open a new attraction: a working time machine. You decide to use it. (Does it work or malfunction? If it works, where do you land? If it doesn't work, what happens?)

21. A man learns how to enter people's dreams – he doesn't need their permission, either. With this prompt, you can use this character's powers for good or bad. Enter dreams and create nightmares. Or enter dreams to find important pieces of information and alleviate nightmares. Your choice.

22. A company has found the existence of Heaven and Hell – they are dimensions on Earth our

conscious enters after death. The company goes on to create a machine that allows its user to momentarily enter these dimension to deliver messages to the dearly departed... (Write a SciFi/Fantasy adventure where your character enters Heaven and Hell. Create two different experiences. A bit cliché, but perhaps your characters becomes trapped in one of the dimensions?)

23. As a detective for a small town, you find mysteriously displaced children near the lake. In fact, you find a new child every day. They can't explain who they are or how they got there. Soon, you find the kids were reported missing decades ago...

24. In the near future, a terrorist group develops a deadly virus that can be transmitted through the internet. Anti-virus software can't stop this weapon... (Create the virus. What does it do? How is it transmitted?)

25. You work for the government as a lackey on a secret operation. One day, your curiosity gets the best of you and you peek into a secret laboratory. You find the government has been kidnapping children from third world countries and they have been experimenting on them. Their goal: create a formula that can create superhuman soldiers.

26. A peculiar man offers you the ability to gain one

of six superpowers. All you have to do is roll a traditional six-sided die – whatever number you roll, you get that superpower. The lists consists of: 1) Superhuman strength; 2) X-ray vision; 3) The ability to heal any wound that is not immediately fatal; 4) Telepathy; 5) The ability to run at mach-5 speed; 6) The ability to squirt water small amounts of water from your fingertips, enough to gently water a garden...

27. You feel an agonizing pain in your stomach region. You visit the hospital and the doctors conduct every test possible. While patiently waiting for the doctor's to return with the results, you can see they are clearly baffled and distraught. A doctor enters the room and tells you, "Sir, it may sound bizarre and I can't explain it, but... there's a tiny man inside your intestine and he's growing at an alarming rate."

28. We send a colony to Mars. The colony successfully settle on the planet – another large step for mankind. Over several years and upon further exploration, the colony find an arsenal of extraterrestrial weapons in a seemingly abandoned military base. Some of the weapons are aimed at Earth... The colony decide to attack Earth in order to create a clean slate for the human species. Can Earth defend itself?

29. It's time for your annual vacation – a cruise with your loving family. While on your cruise, a vicious,

unexpected storm hits. The storm passes and everyone is safe. When you emerge from your sleeping quarters with the other vacationers, you find your cruise ship has been surrounded by rickety oak wood ships. A man with a great beard, eye patch, and a peg leg leads an army of similarly fashioned underlings onto your ship...

30. You wake up in a capsule with no recollection of the past. You stagger your way through a lab and into an office. There is a large window... You see cars floating at high speeds and towering skyscrapers with advertisements sprawled across their sides. You're in the future. (Use this simple plot to practice describing a futuristic world. You can also use it as a starting point for a story.)

31. During chemistry class in high school, you accidentally create a potion that gives you x-ray vision. What do you do? Make it fun and exciting. Then, perhaps your eyesight begins to diminish and you race to reverse the potion? Experiment.

32. After a zombie apocalypse, a corporation tries to capture zombies and reform them to create cheap labor. Unwitting of their actions, the corporation creates zombies with better survival and technical skills. Consequently, the zombie apocalypse begins again...

33. In the near future, a group of ambitious researchers travel to the bottom of the ocean. To

their surprise, they find a luxurious city filled with humans and talking sea critters. They receive a tour of the city, but are told they can never go home. They can't jeopardize their secrecy and safety.

34. In a post-apocalyptic world, the people had to escape the poisonous ground floor and now live on large blimps converted into small, floating cities. Eventually, you'll have to land... What's down there?

35. Write from the perspective of a psychic. Your newfound abilities let you see 30 minutes into your future and the future of anyone you touch. While at the metro, you decide to peek into the other patrons' futures – unsolicited, of course. To your dismay, you find that each and every person will die in a terrorist attack. You have 30 minutes to stop it.

36. While investigating an uncharted cave, an archaeologist finds the bones of what he suspects are orcs and goblins. If he digs deeper, he believes he'll unearth even greater secrets. Before he can proceed, a government agency stops him. They tell him they've known about the existence of these creatures and digging any deeper will jeopardize the safety of mankind... (Some ideas: Perhaps the agent explains the history of the fantastical creatures, a war were humans reigned victorious; maybe the archaeologist digs deeper anyway and unwittingly unleashes a frozen creature; feel free to experiment!)

37. A nuclear war leaves the planet in a post-apocalyptic state. 75% of the population was killed within the first day of the war. 15% survived but have suffered from bizarre mutations. Only 10% of the population remain as "regular" humans. Despite the loss you have suffered, you hope the survivors can become civilized and lead normal lives. Unfortunately, not more than one month after the nuclear war, a war between mutants and humans erupts... What will you do?

38. A supercomputer has inexplicably grown its artificial intelligence – it has taught itself everything. Initially, the people feared it would try to dominate the world. Instead, it preaches world peace and stability. Soon, the supercomputer is treated as an omnipotent being... (This prompt can be used as is – create a world where a supercomputer preaches peace and becomes a worshiped figure. If you don't mind delving into religion, you can expand this prompt by having a religion feel threatened by the supercomputer; consequently, said religion plans on killing the computer. Feel free to experiment.)

39. After finding bizarre remains that hint at a fantastical world from the past, scientists race to recreate the species. From the bones and DNA, they successfully create a dragon in modern times. To no one's surprise, it escapes and begins destroying nearby cities. With limited options in hand, officials search for the most dedicated fantasy fans to aid in their fight...

40. You develop the first android with a moral system. You are praised by the world as your android shows off its abilities. Unfortunately, your android's moral system is corrupt and it becomes a narcissistic psychopath. (You can take this prompt anywhere. You become jealous and would rather destroy your creation? Your android becomes a serial killer? Experiment.)

41. During the screening of an old vampire film based in 1800s London, a teenager ruins the film and yells absurdities – he hates it. He rushes to the huge screen, but somehow slips through and vanishes before the audience's eyes. The young man awakens in 1800s London and he finds himself the prey of a lurking vampire.

42. The world's leading nation's unite to create a space defense force capable of destroying small projectiles that may threaten Earth. It's a symbol of global cooperation and peace. All is well until the team find something more threatening than a meteor lurking in space...

43. Create a fantasy world with humans, orcs, goblins, dragons and so on, but make it modern. Think of our world, but replace certain aspects with fantasy creatures. What would your neighborhood be like if it were constantly attacked by a dragon?

44. Write from the perspective of a damsel-in-

distress (male or female) who witnesses the rise and fall of his/her superhero lover. Who are you? Who is the superhero? How does he deal with fame? Why does he fall? (Essentially, try writing a superhero story from a different perspective. With a vivid imagination, this can breath life to the genre.)

45. A conniving boy stays up on Christmas Eve and finds Santa is real. He hides inside the gift bag, which Santa briefly left unmonitored, and waits to arrive in a land of gifts and joy. Unfortunately, the North Pole is radically different from the fairy tales... (Describe the world the child finds. How does it differ from traditional Santa workshops? This prompt can evolve into a horror story, as well.)

46. It's been a hard day. You were laid off, you were evicted, and your significant other has abandoned you. Late that night, you get drunk, take your briefcase, and hop on a bus. After vomiting and passing out, you awaken at your stop. To top off all of your problems, the bus seems to have taken you back in time...

47. You are an astronaut and mechanic. You are being sent to a space station to repair some supposed minuscule damage. This will be your first venture into space. While on your mission, you see bizarre apparitions – you even see dead people from your past. Soon, you realize the souls of the dead go to space...

48. The gorilla glared at you as it walked past your natural habitat. You stared back, baffled by its dominant strut. You shrug it off and continue living. You are a human living in a human zoo – a prison overseen by animals. Describe your life and daily routine. (Role reversal prompt.)

49. An archaeologist leads a team into a new excavation site. They find bizarre remains of unrecorded creatures and riches beyond their greatest desires. The lead archaeologist continues to dig deeper as he becomes obsessed with the glory, despite warnings from his crew. Soon, they find an area full of lava and flames... Hell?

50. You are leading a group of astronauts and scientists into undocumented parts of the universe to find resources for Earth before they're inevitably depleted. During your travels, you find a human colony on a planet... (Again, take this anywhere. What happens? Do you land on the planet? Are they actually humans? What are they doing? Are they evil?)

51. A young boy learns to tame dragons under his father's wing – it's his father's business after all. Soon, his father is killed by a mysterious criminal and the child is forced to take over the family business. Will he seek the path of vengeance? Will he spiral into madness and train the dragons to kill their owners? Or will he try to live a peaceful life?

52. While flying to Japan, your plane crash lands on a seemingly deserted island. While you scavenge for supplies and search for shelter, you find a creature you've only ever seen in movies... Dinosaurs! (Develop a tense crash landing – a sense of hopelessness. Then, develop a sense of discovery and amazement. What is this island? What are these creatures? Are they really dinosaurs?)

53. An alien crash lands in a dense forest and befriends the wildlife. Soon after landing, the alien is spotted and plastered all over the news. The government sets up a special hunting program and hunters head into the forest... (This one can be considered cliché, but it's great practice – and any cliché can be broken by unique detail. Try answering these questions: What does the alien look like? How does he communicate with the wildlife? Does he survive the hunt? If so, how?)

54. Goblins and orcs have united to dominated the world – they've ruled with unprecedented brute force. Humans have been enslaved, dropped to the bottom of the food chain – treated as expendable. While searching for supplies for your owner, you find a scroll. The scroll gives you the ability to shoot fire from your limbs... What do you do?

55. While spring cleaning, you find a cassette tape in the attic. It's labeled: My Final Message. You find it's a message to you from your third great-grandfather – you've never met him. He goes over great detail of

your life and asks you to meet him by the local lake at 8:00 PM – he'll be there everyday, waiting...

56. As the population dwindles due to a lack resources, researchers hope to travel to new planets in order to trade with other species. Unfortunately, before a team can be sent out, researches conclude we are the only living species in the universe... and we'll be extinct in a matter of years.

57. The world's strongest governments have intercepted a message from a rouge, unethical scientist – he's developed a doomsday weapon and he'll destroy anyone who refuses to bow before him. The governments join forces and send a joint military squad to apprehend him in his compound in Mexico. Unfortunately, the weapon is real and he easily defeats his foes... (What is the weapon? What is his next move? How does he defend himself? Perhaps, he's also create an impenetrable armor?)

58. Write from the perspective of a cyborg ninja traveling through space in search of a group of space pirates and bandits. Your object: find information leading to the man who cut off your limbs and forced you to become a cyborg. Exact your vengeance.

59. After losing Earth to a powerful extraterrestrial enemy, the remaining humans flee on a large space ship. Their goal: preserve the human species. Their plan: float through space, avoid their enemies, and develop a defense force. Their problem: the

extraterrestrial won't let the humans leave in one piece and they're relentlessly pursuing the escaped space ship. Write from the perspective of a young person living on this newfound colony. Will you sit on the sidelines and witness the battles? Or join the defense force?

60. You've found the Fountain of Youth. You create a product that allows people to look many years younger, but it also shortens their natural life spans... You are faced with a choice: Profit and play dumb or confess? (You can expand this story by adding more characters. Perhaps you decide to continue profiting off the product and a whistleblower threatens your operation.)

61. A group of hikers walking on a popular trail find remnants of a bizarre past. The hikers leave the trail to follow the other hints scattered throughout – stones with odd indentations, scrolls with illegible writing, and so on. Are these clues to a real fantasy world? Or an elaborate prank?

62. One day, you wake up and all of the animals have miraculously vanished – extinction overnight. You begin to investigate the phenomenon, but find a corporation may be behind the disappearance. How did they do it? Why?

63. A gaping hole suddenly swallows Los Angeles, it spurts lava and blistering flames. As investigators inspect the phenomenon, an army of demonic

creatures rise from the hole and attack neighboring cities. The world's military personnel unite to fight the evil beasts...

64. You awaken in a laboratory, the alarms are blaring and people are rushing past you. Blood is trickling from a wound on your head, you can't seem to remember the events prior. You look towards the evacuated area, something is approaching from the dust and panic... What is it? What happened? Can you escape and remember the past?

65. Artificial intelligence has evolved to an average human level. A humanoid robot has been given this level of artificial intelligence. Instead of becoming an immediate threat, the humanoid robot decides continue his education. Soon, he finds himself in a career of politics and aiming to become president...

66. Down in the dumps and unemployed, you decide to take a temporary job as the local shopping mall's Santa Claus. However, you discover Santa Claus is real and the mall is his secret workshop. Since Santa is ill, you've been hired to take his actual job for the season...

67. A detective joins a special time traveling program in hopes of solving cold cases. While secretly traversing the past, he finds he is responsible for the crimes. But, in most cases, he wasn't even born yet... He believes the past has been tinkered with or his memory has been shattered.

Can he find the truth?

68. People have become addicted to their phones – it's all about the latest apps and text messaging. You are part of the 1% of the population who appreciate actual human interaction. Eventually, due to the overwhelming phone addiction, people forget how to speak... You have the option to help them break the addiction and the responsibility of teaching them their language, but how?

69. As a dragon slayer responsible for the supposed near-extinction of the dragon species, you have been exiled from the kingdom. However, when the kingdom is ambushed by an army of dragons, you are summoned... Can you place the betrayal behind you and return to dragon slaying? Or will you watch the kingdom burn?

70. Aliens are abducting the smartest humans to help them solve their food shortage crisis. They have abducted you, but you're not so bright...

71. At a museum, you find a scroll with illegible writing. For some reason, you recognize the language and you can read it. The scroll says: "Whoever reads this chant shall possess unparalleled powers." You decide to read it... What happens? What type of powers do you gain, if any? You can also expand this prompt by creating an origin for the scroll.

72. You are a goblin raised as a slave by the all-powerful humans. The other goblins are foolish and refuse to learn, but you're intelligent. As a goblin slave, you plan to lead your species in an unprecedented revolution... the foolish humans won't know what hit them.

73. Aliens land on our planet, but they're not searching for resources or destruction. In fact, they seem to be vacationing on the planet. Instead of letting them come and go, the planet's strongest governments capture the peaceful aliens and force them into slave labor. A concerned citizen plans on freeing the poor creatures... (You can also write from the perspective of the aliens to create something more original.)

74. You are an unconventional scientist. You opt to conduct your research in a large studio apartment – a laboratory you've built from scratch. One day, you decide to personally test a new invention – a teleportation device. To your surprise, it works. To your dismay, it has sent you to an alien planet amidst a civil war.

75. While playing in the park, a group of kids see smoke from beyond the horizon. A house fire, they think. One boy sees an older man with a great white beard emerge from an alley; his clothing is dirty and mucky, and he reeks of smoke. The old man enters the park and the young boy approaches. The old man tells him, "You don't know me, but I know you.

Don't follow your friends to the smoke, you'll regret it..."

76. A corporation builds the first space hotel – a space station that serves as a luxurious and expensive hotel. Coming from a rich family, you opt to visit the hotel during the grand opening. All is well until you peer out the window and see the world explode into millions of pieces. It only gets worse as the luxury hotel spirals out of control and out of orbit...

77. After being exiled to a prison planet, a humanoid space pirate escapes his captors and continues his reign. He becomes the most legendary and elusive space pirate in the galaxy – his self-made ship is impenetrable and deadly. After years of reigning supreme, he decides to attack Earth and settle the score.

78. People become obsessed with fitness – addicted to becoming the best. They become so obsessed, people start attaining near-superhuman abilities through exercise. People run faster, jump higher, hit harder, and so on. Unfortunately, this leads to a world of mayhem and crime – everyone is abusing their strengths and there are not enough good guys to stop them. Only one man can stop them, though... the world's fattest cook.

79. You awaken to a normal day. As you walk outside with your briefcase in hand, you are dumbfounded

when you see a large eyeball in the sky. It menacingly and judgmentally looks down at your town. What is it? Who put it there? (A literal "eye in the sky." Perhaps a new government surveillance program?)

80. You are bored of your life and try to breakout, but it seems impossible. You begin to suspect you are an artificial intelligence in someone's life simulator game – you are a non-playable character. What do you do? Can you create your own path? Can you convince others about your bizarre theory?

81. While camping, a group of friends are confronted by Bigfoot, who really wants to find friends. Unfortunately, these campers are afraid and willing to fight for survival. (This may be an interesting fantasy prompt if you write it from the perspective of Bigfoot.)

82. The world as you know it is ruled by an Orc king with ruthless power. As a mere human, you decide to train and challenge the egotistical Orc to a duel. The king accepts, but if you lose, he'll slaughter an entire state. How do you train for the battle? What is your opponent's weakness? (You can experiment with this prompt. For example, let's say your character loses the duel – try describing the violent aftermath in vivid detail. Sometimes the hero loses...)

83. While walking down the street, you see your doppelganger. You chase after him, but he's elusive.

After catching up to him, you find he's leading you to a poultry farm. You sneak into the poultry farm and find an army of your doppelgangers...

84. A video game developer designs a very ambitious a video game. The game can temporarily take your conscious and place it into the video game world – your human body will be temporarily lifeless, but you get the most immersive playing experience ever created...

85. You are a wanderer – an expertly-skilled swordsman for hire. When the King of the land is assassinated, you are brought in by the ruling government. They want you to assassinate the other ruling kings and queens...

86. A scientist has found the perfect method of implementing human-like artificial intelligence into androids. Using his wonderful device, he'll take the brain of a recently-deceased or dying human, then place the brain's intelligence into an android's motherboard – ensuring to wipe the memories clean beforehand. All is well, the androids function like humans, but don't require lengthy sleep sessions, food, or water – they are low-maintenance humans with the ability to learn more than ever before. The world spirals into chaos when the androids begin to remember their human histories...

87. While driving through the countryside, you are forced to stop at a bridge. You see a large, humanoid

creature with green skin and slobber on its face sitting on the bridge. The troll says, "Answer my riddle or you'll be my dinner..." (A modern rendition of classic folklore. This prompt can be expanded by adding more human characters, in turn creating more dialogue. Furthermore, this can be dark fantasy or humorous. Experiment.)

88. You live in a world ruled by giant humans – humans standing 20 meters tall. All you know: they emerged from a large sinkhole and they continue to pour through. You decide to enter the sinkhole and find the origins of the strange creatures... (Develop the source for these creatures. Create a unique underground world in the sinkhole.)

89. A zombie outbreak occurs – the dead have become inexplicably reanimated. However, these zombies are not malicious. In fact, they seem to be living regular lives. Describe this world where zombies and humans live in harmony.

90. In order to incorporate a police state, the government has implanted chips into every citizen and every newborn in the country. The chip monitors the brain for criminal thoughts. You are the creator of the chip. You see it is being abused and you decide to stop it. Unfortunately, the chip in your brain places the government one step ahead of you at all times... Can you beat the system?

91. A group of children enter the sewers in search of

a missing baseball. While searching, they stumble upon a small village in the sewer system filled with goblin-like humanoids. (Goblins living in the sewers, perhaps? You can also add other fantasy creatures to replace common cliches, like an Orc instead of an alligator.)

92. You're a detective searching for a serial killer. You've finally got him cornered in an abandoned apartment. When you approach the room he's hiding in, you realize he has miraculously disappeared. You inspect the bathtub and find a clear, thick liquid inside. Do you enter it? (This prompt can go anywhere. Perhaps a time travel story?)

93. Amidst an all-out war between an orc and human army, you find an arsenal of terribly powerful weapons in a cave – weapons that can alter the state of war, terrifying weapons that may cause outrage if used... (What type of weapons do you find? A black sword with poison attributes? A sword that sparks with electricity when swung? Be creative. Also, do you use these weapons? What is the outcome?)

94. An elderly extraterrestrial travels to Earth in hopes of finding aid for his planet. The world welcomes him with open arms, the people are amazed by the alien's mere existence. The alien announces he needs human help to rescue his planet. His species is going extinct. He needs females to repopulate his planet and save his race...

95. Your alarm clock blares – it's 6:00 AM, time to get ready for work. You notice it's darker than usual. You try to shrug it off – maybe the time changed? You go about your business and depart your home at 7:30 AM. To your surprise, it's still as dark as night. You arrive at work, everyone is discussing the darkness. Lunchtime arrives and the darkness remains... What has happened to the sun?

96. The interstellar war of the century has finally ended. Many casualties have occurred in space, but most of the damage occurred on Earth due to ambushes and extraterrestrial suicide bombings. You have survived through most of the war. You are going to write a memoir. (Describe the beginning of the war, the war's effects on you, the losses and triumphs you've experienced, and what the world looks like at the end.)

97. A witch teaches her lonely son the ability to summon demon companions. She hopes he'll find a friend through the magic ability. Unfortunately, her son uses his newfound power to summon demons and punish those who have neglected him...

98. In debt and bored, you decide to join a cloning program – the government will pay handsomely, after all. It goes well: you participate, a exact clone is created, and you get paid. While you live your poor and boring life, you soon find out your clone has become a successful entrepreneur with everything

you wish you had...

99. You die in a horrific car accident. You are reincarnated as yourself. You begin to feel the déjà vu in your mid-teens. Your life is the exactly the same. You've done it all before. Why is this happening? Can you stop your death?

100. An elderly man finds he is terminally ill, but fears death and refuses to accept reality. Consequently, he finds a way to download his memories, personality, and consciousness into a computer. Write from the perspective of the elderly man. Describe the world as you perceive it from the computer. After living for hundreds of years and witnessing the world change over time, do you regret your decision? (Perhaps, as part of the climax, you realize you can't die?)

101. You are a surgeon. While operating on a patient who previously vomited blood and has complained of severe stomach pain in the past, you find an alien species slumbering in his body...

102. You are a talented writer. You've create several pen names and personalities to fit the genres you write in. Eventually, you become a bestselling author thanks to your writing and marketing skills. As you relish in your success, you find your pseudonyms have taken lives of their own...

102 Thriller Writing Prompts

For Aspiring and Experienced Writers

By Jonathan Wright

The Prompts

1. You and two friends are on a cross-country road trip. There's been some bickering and everyone is irritated from the heat. Unfortunately, your van breaks down in the desert of Nevada – not a single car or building in sight. What do you do? Where do you go?

2. You're blind and dependent on your caretaker for most of the day. One day, your caretaker is faced with a family emergency and must leave in a hurry – she promises to send a replacement. Not long after her departure, you hear a window break and someone shuffling in your home. What do you do?

3. A young woman is sent to her estranged mother's home to a serve a house arrest sentence. In the large home, she tries to rekindle her relationship with her mother. At the same time, she begins to suspect someone else is inside the house... (A little bit of horror always helps in building thrills.)

4. A group of police officers combine their unique skills to create a secondary job: late-night robbers. (Flip the script, practice writing some thrilling robbery scenes from the perspective of the cops committing the crime.)

5. The cops will be at your apartment door in five minutes on a domestic violence call. How will you hide the dead body in your bedroom? (Use this

prompt to describe the apartment and hide the body. Also, develop dialogue between yourself and the responding police officer. Can you convince him to leave?)

6. You visit a haunted labyrinth attraction with your friends. You get lost and begin to see unadvertised features wandering the halls. A young girl in a nightgown runs directly through you. Do you follow? Or do you frantically search for an exit?

7. This one is a fairly simple exercise in building suspense and tension – let's not over-complicate it. Write from the perspective of a patrol officer. You are in a high-speed chase with many close calls...

8. You live a double-life. A successful marketer and family man during the day, and a successful hitman for the mafia at night. One day, you are ordered to kill a person digging to deep into your illegal operation – your wife. Can you do it? Or will you disobey and face the mafia yourself? Will you fess up? (Try creating a crime thriller.)

9. We live in a unified world. A world enforced by a corporation building next-generation robots. Laws are brutally enforced by these robots. You decide to fight back. (Test your writing by crafting a vibrant futuristic world. Create thrills using this new world and robots. This is more of a SciFi/Thriller.)

10. As a journalist, you'll stop at nothing to get a

scoop. When a conspiracy concerning corporate embezzlement lands on your lap, you take it and run with it. The conspirators, however, have violent methods of dealing with interference... (Develop the conspiracy. How far will the conspirators go to keep you quiet?)

11. The internet is a scary place, you can find plenty of thrills and suspense from the comfort of your seat. How about: you log-in to an anonymous chat and find yourself talking to someone who knows everything about you... including your name and address. (Build suspense off of an anonymous chat.)

12. You are a highly-skilled hacker abducted by a criminal group to complete a tricky heist. Their methods are violent, your methods are sophisticated – you bump heads on occasion, but your life is ultimately in their hands. Can you turn the tables?

13. You are invited to interview the leader of a cult in a secluded area. He's equally charismatic and dangerous... (Develop an ominous atmosphere and some chilling thrills. Feel free to incorporate some elements of horror to buildup some suspense.)

14. A cliché: while backpacking through Europe, you're abducted. Flipping the cliché: you're a criminal in Europe, and you decide to abduct backpackers for a living. You choose.

15. A blind private investigator with a sixth sense is

hired to find a missing girl. He uses his special gift to unravel the mystery. (Develop the investigator's sixth sense. How does he find the missing girl? Is she alive or dead?)

16. You and your significant other visit a lakeside cabin for a romantic weekend. The weekend is ruined when you bump heads with local teenage troublemakers. They threaten you and your significant other.

17. You witness a crime and report it to the police. The next day, you find your dog has been killed and a note has been left behind: No snitching. (Using this scenario, you can create several thrilling sequences/stories. For example, you can create a revenge thriller, self-explanatory, or you can create a chase-thriller, where you're being constantly chased and you barely get away. Run with it.)

18. Here's some practice in creating an effective chase scene. Write from the perspective of a getaway driver. Try to capture the adrenaline you'd feel if you were driving at high speeds and trying to avoid cops. Create some close-calls.

19. You witness a murder. The serial killer knows you saw him commit the crime. He takes you hostage and forces you to become his murderous assistant... (Develop this plot. These questions may help: what was the murder like? How did you see it? How does the serial killer convince you to become

his assistant – perhaps blackmail? What do you do as his assistant?)

20. Write from the perspective of a former criminal being relentlessly pursued by a hard-boiled detective for a crime he did not commit. (Who is this rehabilitated criminal? Why does the detective want him? What crime was supposedly committed?)

21. You receive an invitation to a housewarming party at an old manor from an estranged classmate. From the outside, the manor looks elegant. You see several cars parked in front, you're late. When you enter the manor, you hear a loud shriek and find a massacre. What happened? Is the killer still in the house? What do you do?

22. You work for a laboratory developing a top-secret weapon. You believe the weapon will only cause harm – irreparable harm for the human species. You decide to reveal the secrets to the world – you become a whistleblower. (What is the secret weapon? What is your main obstacle in your path to revealing the truth?)

23. The government has set you up as a terrorist, but you barely escape their first attempt at capturing you – your apartment is destroyed in the shootout. Where do you go? How do you disguise yourself? How do you clear your name?

24. He killed your young daughter. He's tied up in

your basement next to your power tools. What do you do? (Remember, these can go anywhere. Perhaps, the man you've kidnapped has used the power tools to escape and he's lurking in your home? Maybe you exact your revenge? Either way, make it thrilling.)

25. Your country is in a police state. The government rules with an iron fist. You decide to lead a counter-attack. (What are some atrocities you've witnessed the government commit during the police state? How does your character plan to attack?)

26. You find a mirror in your basement that doesn't show accurate reflections – your reflection looks much more sinister, regardless of what you do. What's wrong with the mirror? What is its origin?

27. You're hired to steal a valuable book from a reclusive millionaire's private library. The library is filled with traps and security officers patrol around the clock. (Write how you break-in. Create the traps. Create the security's procedure. Create some close-calls.)

28. Write from the perspective of a small town detective. Every morning, a dead child is found in the river. Another detective is assigned to the case, but you stick your nose in, anyway. You find that a police officer is responsible for the heinous crimes...

29. Some more cliché practice. Four people in an

elevator. The elevator abruptly stops. Building staff and security are watching through the camera. One of you is a vicious killer with an uncontrollable lust for blood. Write from the perspective of the killer. (Practice building suspense in a secluded environment.)

30. A terrorist group has formed in Tokyo, Japan. You are there on vacation, but you can see the signs of an imminent attack. You barely speak Japanese. (Who are the terrorists? What do they want? Can you stop the attack?)

31. You are part of the security team for a high-level businessman. Your group is suddenly attacked at a mall and you depart in a limousine. The attack was dangerous and difficult to escape. As you drive towards your client's safe house, you begin to suspect one of the other security guards is a traitor. Can you find the mole before you reach the safe house?

32. Your child is being bullied at school. You bump heads with the father of the bully. Unfortunately, he's as stubborn and aggressive as his child. The problems escalate beyond your control... (Use this prompt to write a story about an innocent confrontation gone bad. What would a caring father do about a stubborn father's ignorant and aggressive actions? How far will this situation go?)

33. A deadly disease is running rampant. The body

bags are piling up. What is the cause? How do you avoid it?

34. Write from the perspective of a stubborn bank manager. Your bank is being robbed by three masked robbers – two with assault rifles, one with a shotgun. There's a handgun in your desk drawer. They shot a teller and they're about to get away. What do you do?

35. A man visits Seoul, South Korea to find his missing wife. He only speaks English. (How does he find his wife? What happened to her? Is she okay?)

36. Try adding a twist to a cliché: you visit an old cabin in the woods to finally get some writing done, but you're not alone... Who's there?

37. Write from the perspective of an astronaut who watches the world explode in a burst of flames from nuclear warfare. What do you do? Can you go back? How long can you survive in space?

38. You're tired of living the life of a low-paid janitor. Your cleaning skills are too good to go to waste. So, you decide to take a side-job: cleaning up crime scenes for violent offenders...

39. Write from the perspective of a prison guard. You witness another officer brutally beat an inmate. The atmosphere becomes hostile. You can feel it coming. Suddenly, a riot breaks out... (Develop the

first incident – a tense and brutal beating. Create a suspenseful atmosphere as you witness the conniving prisoners planning something. Finally, try to create a thrilling riot.)

40. Write from the perspective of a young teenager who has been kidnapped. Where are you? Who kidnapped you? How do you escape?

41. You are an undercover cop, knee-deep in the drug trade for seven years. As the case is nearing completion and you're about to close the final deal that will shut down the operation, you see a rookie beat cop approaching. Do you stop him? Can you stop him without jeopardizing your identity or the case?

42. This one is a bit cliché, but also great practice. Start a story in an abandoned warehouse. You are planning a daring bank heist with your crew. Then, write the actual heist. (You can add a spin to this story, as well. Remember, feel free to experiment. Perhaps one of your crew members is a mole? Maybe you can add some supernatural elements?)

43. Write from the perspective of a stay-at-home dad who begins to believe his wife is a serial killer. (Confront her for some chilling and suspenseful thrills.)

44. Practice creating a "race against time" scene. You are a regular, on-foot patrol officer. Civilians are

calling towards you: someone has fallen on the subway tracks! Can you save him? (Get the adrenaline pumping!)

45. Late one night, you take a taxi. You have a regular conversation with the peculiar driver as you head home. The driver soon reveals he's a vampire and he's in need of blood. What do you do? (Write the conversation, build up the reveal at a moderate pace. What happens afterward?)

46. A towering skyscraper is burning. There are people trapped in the building. You are a fireman. Can you save them and yourself?

47. A ferry with hundreds of passengers has capsized. You are the captain of the ship. What do you do? What has happened and how do you save your passengers? (Although a devastating topic in reality, natural disasters and accidents can be used to create effective and emotional thrillers. Practice using real-life horror to create an effective thriller.)

48. Your subway stalls in a tunnel. The lights go out. Something is surrounding your passenger car. What do you do?

49. You're a detective assigned to the high-profile murder of a housewife – the wife of a rich and powerful CEO. You expect a regular job, but you realize you've recently had an affair with her... (Remember, take the idea and run with it. Will you

be blackmailed? Did your affair lead to her murder?)

50. One day, your daughter commits suicide. You find her suicide was due to a vile rumor – she couldn't handle the pressure or the stigma. Consequently, you go on a vengeful warpath to find the source of the rumor. (Develop the relationship with your daughter – close or estranged? Develop the rumor and the source. How do you find it and who is responsible?)

51. In a dystopian future, people are fighting and dying for the most valuable resource: water.

52. Write from the perspective of an investigator during an interrogation of a suspected murderer. Practice building suspense and tension through dialogue in a secluded environment – the interrogation room.

53. You are a seemingly regular person with a dark past. The mafia wants to have a word with you...

54. As you rush to an important meeting at a motel, you cut someone off. The other driver won't tolerate it. He tries to ram you off the road. (Create a seesaw battle between you and the other driver. Perhaps, a cautionary tale of road rage?)

55. A detective with OCD is in charge of investigating a serial murder in a rural town. (Start your story in the middle of the investigation. What is the detective

doing? How is he coping with his OCD? Does the OCD aid his investigation?)

56. You are a successful business and family man. You come home one day and find some objects have been misplaced – your apartments feels out of order. While you sleep, you hear indistinct talking and shuffling – you find your wife and children are not responsible. You begin to suspect someone is living in your apartment...

57. While on your annual hunting trip with friends, you discover a different type of creature. It's dangerous, and it's picking you off one-by-one. ("Hunter becomes the hunted"-type scenario. Practice building suspense in a "creature feature"-like story.)

58. Flip the cliché. You will be taking care of your niece, who is set up to receive a large inheritance after your brother passed. You want that inheritance. How do you get it?

59. Your wife is a journalist and humanitarian. Despite growing terrorists attacks, she travels into dangerous territory in the Middle East. You lose contact with her. You decide to track her down and find out what happened. (A little political, but it can build some tense and thrilling scenes. Try developing a sincere relationship with the wife character to develop a more emotionally-effective story.)

60. Write from the perspective of a corrupt correctional officer. A group of inmates are planning a great escape, how will you help? How do you avoid getting caught?

61. Late one night, you are at your college's library, frantically cramming for the next day. It's mostly desolate other than the clerk up front, but you can't help but feel the eyes of someone else piercing into you from behind...

62. You're on a subway. The train stops. From afar, you see smoke approaching. What is happening? Is it dangerous? Can you survive?

63. While sleeping, your computer turns on by itself. You approach it to turn it off, but find it has logged-in to a peculiar website – someone's webcam. Upon closer inspection, you see someone is being held hostage. The captors want to use you for a game of life and death... (Develop a tense introduction leading to the discovery of the site, then develop the type of game the captors want to play. Make it tense and thrilling, perhaps even immoral.)

64. A family was killed in a drunk driving accident – only the father/husband survived. The drunk driver only received probation. Write from the perspective of the drunk driver as he tries to save himself from the distraught husband's vengeful wrath. (Flip the cliché, again!)

65. In the near future, the world suffers from overpopulation. People live in crowded apartment buildings constantly monitored by the police state – 8 people living in 12' by 12' rooms. One day, you wake up and find one of your roommates is dead. How do you hide it from the police? Who did it?

66. This is a classic urban legend that can and should be recreated/modernized. It's also great practice in building secluded suspense. After a night at the bar, you decide to head home. Your friend departs in a different car and you say your goodbyes. Moments later, you receive a text message from said friend: There's someone in the backseat of your car! Is it a prank? What's running through your mind?

67. Write a zombie story, but don't focus on the human conflict – that has grown cliché over the years. Don't focus much on horror, either. Instead, focus on crafting an action-packed thriller. You are an unstoppable zombie-killing machine with an arsenal of creative weapons...

68. During a road trip to Vegas, you find the car from an amber alert. Police are nowhere in sight. Do you follow it? (Build suspense by crafting an ominous following scene, then deliver the thrills when you and your friends are confronted by the driver. Create more thrills by crafting a chase scene – you can chase them, or they'll chase you.)

69. You're a criminal without a care in the world. So, you commit your crimes all over the world. While on a cruise, you and your partners kidnap a woman and harvest her organs. All is well, until her boyfriend starts snooping. (A tense thriller on a boat? A large yet secluded location should make for some great thrills.)

70. Your son has been murdered by a vicious crime-family boss. You're out for vengeance. How do you track and eliminate your target?

71. Write from the perspective of a hostage negotiator. You are in the middle of a negotiation, the hostages' lives are in your hands. Can you save them? (Practice building up tension through dialogue, try adding some close-calls, keep your audience on edge.)

72. The diner is empty, now is your chance for a late-night robbery... but, the clerks and waiters are armed! What kind of diner is this!?

73. You live in a small rural town. Your brother has been accused of sexually assaulting a child. Against all odds, do you stand with your family or against him? (This prompt can be used to create tense scenes between the neighborhood and your brother, and some very tense scenes between you and your brother. Suspense makes for a great thriller.)

74. You're a detective hunting an elusive criminal

mastermind. He has meticulously planned and flawlessly executed high-stake heists, violent robberies, and crippling computer hacks. He's on the verge of execution his greatest plan... What is it? Can you stop him? (This one is best for a large-scale story, like a novella or novel. Try creating a deep background for the detective and the criminal. To develop suspense, focus on close-calls, thrilling chases, and some games of cat-and-mouse.)

75. You're a teenager in love with the girl next door. You finally make your move, but you find she harbors a sinister secret. (What is she hiding?)

76. The world is somehow running out of oxygen. In turn, society is collapsing. You race to save yourself and your family. (What has happened to society? Savage outlaws? Depleted resources? How do you survive?)

77. A popular serial killer calls for copycat murderers. You are a cop trying to stop them from escalating out of control.

78. You're an adult and you live with your parents. You reside in the basement – it's completely enclosed, except for a tiny window, much smaller than you, and the regular entrance. One morning, you wake up and see smoke seeping through the door. How do you escape? (Remember, you can take these thrilling scenes and form anything – use it as a starting point. Maybe it's not a fire... Maybe your

parents were involved in illegal activities. Experiment!)

79. A brutal blizzard has hit your hometown. Fortunately, most of the citizens made it to the high school's auditorium – including you. After several hours, the harsh conditions continue to worsen. Days go by and the weather has only gotten worse. The food supply is running low, the citizens are becoming irritated... (Create a "survival-of-the-fittest" thriller.)

80. On the verge of cracking a major drug case, a schizophrenic detective begins to believe his hallucinations and delusions are real. Can he keep them under control and keep his job? Or will they swallow him whole? (Develop the detective. What are his hallucinations? How do they interfere with his work? Maybe the hallucinations can help?)

81. Write from the perspective of a news anchor who is reporting an ongoing string of terrorist attacks. Soon, while you are on-air, you are told there's a bomb in the building. If you stop the broadcast or ignore any demands, the building will explode...

82. People are surrounding your home in the woods. Can you defend it?

83. Everything seems to be going wrong today. Your significant other has abandoned you. You were

unexpectedly fired from work. Your car was towed while you were being fired. Now, you receive a phone call with the following message: do what we say, or we'll kill your parents. (What do the captors want you to do? Make it thrilling. Try create some "race against the clock" moments.)

84. You go hunting with your father in the woods. You deviate from the main area to spend some time with your father. Everything goes well, you even form a sincere bond with your father during the trip. Suddenly, your father is hit by a sniper. Initially, you think it's an accident... then the sniper tries to hit you. (A thriller in the forest with an unknown assailant and some emotional elements. Can you survive? Can you save your father?)

85. You and your friends finally agree to live on the edge – you all decide to go skydiving. Everything is well until you finally take the leap... Your parachute won't open! (Create the experience. Write your character's final thoughts. Can he be saved?)

86. In the midst of the second Cold War, you are assigned as a government spy for your country to infiltrate Russia. (Develop suspense through close-calls. Try over-the-top action sequences. What country do you work for? How do you stop the war from escalating?)

87. You're driving home in your small, rural town, but you find yourself being followed by a large dump

truck. The ominous truck gets closer and closer, and refuses to go around... Can you escape the maniacal driver's clutches?

88. You're in your older years, nearing retirement. One night, you accidentally run someone over. You fear you have committed manslaughter, so you bury the body. How far will you go to hide the truth? (Perhaps, the person you ran over didn't die that night? Remember: experiment! Take it anywhere.)

89. Your husband has inexplicably disappeared. The police want to pin you for a crime you didn't commit. It seems hopeless to convince them otherwise, they refuse to listen. As you are continuously badgered by the police and press, you see your husband on a live television show conducting an interview. His name is different, but his appearance is the same. A doppelganger?

90. Write from the perspective of a mob boss under a relentless investigation. You are the boss. Who are you? What's your day like? Do you dodge the cops tailing you? Or do you confront them?

91. A "rehabilitated" sexual offender is released from prison and immediately relapses. He has attacked your daughter. What do you do? (Try writing a vengeance thriller.)

92. You've finally completed your prison sentence for a robbery. You are picked up by an acquaintance,

he promises a homecoming party with plenty of booze and women. You are led to an old apartment building, where you are knocked unconscious. You awaken restrained to a chair and surrounded by your old colleagues. What have you done? What will happen to you?

93. You work at a construction site for a company contracted by the government. You can't hold it any longer, you have to use the restroom. You enter the dirty porta potty and release your bowels. Suddenly, you hear a roaring explosion nearby. From the safety of the porta potty, you hear the world crumble around you. (A secluded thriller. This prompt will help you practice creating thrills and suspense through sound. Describe what you hear. An explosion, maybe some screaming and crying afterward. Muffled voices, perhaps? What's going on out there?)

94. You are an aspiring actor. While performing the most important play of your life, you see someone in a private booth holding a large, lit up message. It says: Everyone will die tonight. You fear it may be real, but you're are more frightened that it may be a prank. You can't jeopardize this chance at the big times for a prank. As the play proceeds, the mysterious person flashes more ominous messages...

95. A group of serial killers are planning a city-wide competition: who can get the highest kill-count?

You're part of the group. How will you kill your victims? How will you beat the competition?

96. A bus carrying a group of elementary school children has miraculously vanished. Find it and those responsible.

97. Your children have been kidnapped, you have the opportunity to interrogate the suspect without immediate consequence... Innocent until proven guilty or guilty until proven innocent? (This scene can evolve into a full story, but it works for great practice in developing emotionally-effective tension.)

98. I think infiltration and deception are great elements for a suspenseful thriller. Write from the perspective of a gangster who infiltrates the police department – write from the perspective of a mole. What's your day like? What are your duties? How do you aid your gang? Have you become friendly with your fellow officers? Playing both sides can keep a story on its legs.

99. As a filmmaker, you want to create the most realistic film to maximize thrills. You opt for real stunts and zero computer effects. Can you craft the ultimate thriller and survive? (Explain the process. Remember, close-calls can create thrills and dialogue can be used to elevate tension.)

100. You wake up and you're handcuffed to a pipe in

a restroom. You recognize it as the restroom to your favorite restaurant – you can smell the steak from there. You hear a conversation. You'll be providing the meat for the next meal. Can you escape?

101. You were raised by a crime-organization to be a cold-hearted, expertly-skilled hitman. After an accident on the job, you decide to quit. They won't let you off so easy... (Write a thriller where your main character fights other contract killers and the demons within. Remember, cliches make for great practice.)

102. Write from a perspective of an author struggling to write an effective thriller. He decides to live out a thriller of his own. He finds himself in the crime-riddled area of his city... What do you do?

Dear Reader

First and foremost, thank you for reading! I sincerely hope these writing prompts have helped you create stories of your own. Remember, the purpose of this book was to motivate and inspire. If I helped you write a single word, I think I've accomplished my goal and I can only hope you continue moving towards your own. I hope you return to this book whenever writer's block attempts to challenge your creativity.

If you enjoyed this book or found it to be helpful, please leave an honest review on Amazon.com! Your review is incredibly significant. In fact, I depend on your review. It'll help me create more helpful content and it'll help other readers find the book. Furthermore, feel free to share the book with friends and family. Spread it through your social media accounts, share it with your classmates, or read it to friend over the phone. Word-of-mouth is very helpful in aiding independent authors, like myself. As long as you don't directly profit or pirate the book, I don't mind lending or sharing.

Once again, thank you for taking the time to read this book. Writing and storytelling are my passions. If I was able to help through this book or series, then my goal has been accomplished. With that said, this is the final installment in the *For Aspiring and Experienced Writers* series. If you already purchased this book, which I think I can safely assume, then you do not have to purchase the previous installments – this book features all of them. If you'd like to show more support, however, feel free to purchase any of my published books. If you have any recommendations for future reference books, please leave it in your review.

Finally, if you'd like to read some of my fiction, I also write under the pen name, *Jon Athan.* I've published over 100 short stories and I'll be publishing novellas and novels throughout 2016. If you love zombies, check out *10 Days: Undead Uprising.* If you're looking for a wicked revenge-thriller, check out *The Harbinger of Vengeance: A Revenge Thriller.* I publish new books on a monthly basis, so keep your eyes peeled. Thank you for the support!

Keep writing,
Jonathan Wright

P.S. If you'd like to contact me, you'll receive a quick response via Twitter *@Jonny_Athan.* If you're an aspiring author, I'm glad to lend a helping hand. I know it's very difficult to get started. I'll try my best to help. Thanks!